W9-BQS-172

# SMALL GATHERINGS

## SEASONAL MENUS FOR COZY DINNERS

JESSICA STRAND
photographs by Sheri Giblin

EGG & DART PRESS

ACKNOWLEDGMENTS

This part of the book is always the easiest, since you feel indebted to so many people when putting together a project, but it's the trickiest too, you don't want to leave a soul out. I had a wonderful team working on this book. It's they who put together this collection, without them the book would not be here, would not look the way it does in type, design or pictures. The recipes would be moderately confusing at times and the experience of the book would be wholly different. A very special thank you to Publisher Pamela Falk for making this book happen! I owe many, many thanks and dinners to Leslie Jonath, the creative brain and champion behind this project. And to the brilliant managing of this text from the first step to the last, Lisa McGuinness, you were patient, gentle and terrific, many thanks!!! The visionaries—in design, Gretchen Scoble, whose work astonishes me time and time again, and the photographer Sheri Giblin, who made everything from a chicken to a Branzino look gorgeous! Additionally, I'd like to thank food stylist, Paul Lowe and prop stylist, Sarah Cave whose delicate, tasteful, elegant styling helped to create the look of this book.

This book would definitely not exist without my personal team. I had two testers who were brilliant, professional, and simply the best, thank you Kate Garber and Kat Craddock. And as always, I have to thank my tall, affectionate, wonderful son who is the light of my life, thank you Lucian.



ISBN 987-09841887-9-6

Manufactured in China

Designed by Gretchen Scoble

10 9 8 7 6 5 4 3 2

EGG&DART PRESS

www.egganddartpress.com

To my friends, my family,

and all those whom I have fed and

who love to eat

## TABLE OF CONTENTS

# FALL

## DINNER FOR TWO 78



## DINNER FOR FOUR 88



## DINNER FOR SIX 98



# WINTER

## DINNER FOR TWO 112



## DINNER FOR FOUR 120



## DINNER FOR SIX 128

# INTRODUCTION

When I think of food, my mind tends right away to conjure up my favorites—steak, bitter greens, fresh tomatoes, corn, figs, bittersweet chocolate. That is, I don't think of my favorite dishes so much as I think about the ingredients that go into preparing them. Then, from images of beloved foods, my thoughts quickly move to beloved friends. I can't think about food without thinking about those with whom I love to eat: What does Margaret like? What does Tracy love? What could I serve Joseph besides beef and pork? Natalie likes bitter greens with citrus. Lucian likes corn soup.

All meals are more delicious with family and friends. To ooh and aah with your loved ones at the dinner table over perfectly cooked fish or succulent spare-ribs is to experience each other at a whole new level. A chorus of happy eaters elevates shopping, cooking, and even cleaning up to the ranks of life's great pleasures.

This cookbook, like the others I wrote before it, strives to define a straightforward, anxiety-free approach for home cooks, this time to preparing for small dinner parties for from two to six people. My goal was to deliver a combination of delicious, reliable recipes and guidelines on timing and preparation that adds up to a party involving as little stress as possible.

Now, that's not to say that this book guarantees your evening will be completely glitch-free; I mean, things always happen, which is part of the wonderful unpredictable nature of life. But if you follow the details within the following pages, at least you won't have to worry that your almonds will burn, or whether or not your pork is too rare, or about stranding your guests hungry, waiting. The helpful boxes called Menu Managers provide major support with orchestrating the timing of menus covering an entire evening of entertaining, so that you can avoid stress, panic, and/or being buried at the last moment.

The twelve menus in this collection are organized into four chapters representing the seasons of the year, with dinners for two, four, and six in each. When you cook seasonally, you give yourself the great advantage of being able to find the best-quality ingredients at their tastiest. I also put together a list of full-time pantry ingredients that are sure to simplify entertaining when you have them on hand. And I added a short list of perishable ingredients to keep stocked in your refrigerator at all times; these will arm you for creative home cooking for yourself and your family throughout the week, as well as for feeding guests in a spontaneous moment.

So dip into this book and begin to plan your small gatherings: let your dinner-party soul be soothed and stirred by Roasted Spareribs with Homemade Barbecue Sauce (page 104); earthy Wild Mushroom Risotto (page 91); and Raw Summer Squash Salad with French Feta and Toasted Pine Nuts (page 70). For dessert, don't miss Pistachio-Cardamom Cake with Lime Syrup (page 39) or the rosé-poached peaches with crème fraîche (page 62). As you turn the pages, think of your friends dipping cherries into warm homemade chocolate sauce, or of your uncle smiling after a creamy bite of whipped parsnips. All of these meals will delight and yes, create those cries of delight.

More than anything, I hope that this book inspires you to gather your friends and cook a meal you can share with them. With each season comes a different type of gathering. When spring comes around, we want fresh green vegetables sprinkled with bright herbal notes on the palate like mint and marjoram. In summertime, it's a treat to eat outdoors, and most of us have a taste for fresh crunchy vegetables and the clean, distinct flavors produced by the summer heat. In the fall, we suddenly begin to crave something hearty; and in the winter, the cozier and more comforting the food, the better.

May all of your small gatherings be easy and relaxing to prepare. Enjoy!

## WHAT TO HAVE IN YOUR PANTRY AND REFRIGERATOR YEAR-ROUND

Here is a list of items to strive to keep on hand, to make every meal you plan much easier to shop for, and covering you for spontaneous meals anytime. As a bonus, keeping even just a few of these stocked at home will spare you from ever having to worry about being able to cook something if all the stores are closed!

### PANTRY

- Beans and legumes: black, red, navy, or cannellini, split peas, lentils
- Bread crumbs, dried
- Broth: good-quality low-sodium chicken, beef, vegetable
- Chocolate: bittersweet, semisweet chips
- Crackers: crowd-pleasers, artisanal crackers, something unique and crisp
- Dried mushrooms
- Dried herbs and spices: ground cumin, oregano, thyme, cayenne, paprika, curry powder, red pepper flakes, bay leaves, a variety of salts, black peppercorns
- Extracts: almond, vanilla, lemon, orange, mint
- Garlic, fresh and granulated
- Ginger, fresh and powdered
- Grains: rice, barley, quinoa
- Mustard: dry, Dijon, stone-ground, honey-flavored
- Nuts: Walnuts, pistachios, almonds, pine nuts
- Oats, old-fashioned rolled
- Oil: olive, canola, peanut
- Onions: yellow, red, sweet
- Pasta: some strand (spaghetti, linguine) and some shaped (penne, bow-tie)
- Shallots
- Sugar: granulated, brown, coarse
- Tomato paste, canned tomatoes, whole and crushed
- Vinegars: balsamic, sherry, champagne
- White wine

### REFRIGERATOR

- Butter: salted and unsalted
- Eggs
- Fresh thyme
- Milk
- Tarragon
- Parmesan
- Whole Greek yogurt
- Soy sauce
- Dijon mustard
- Anchovies
- Tomato paste (in a tube)
- Capers
- White wine

SPRING

# SPRING DINNER FOR 2

SPRING PEA SOUP WITH MINT AND TOASTED PISTACHIOS

SALMON WITH DILL EN PAPILLOTE

ROASTED FINGERLING POTATOES WITH HERB-AND-LEMON YOGURT

FRESH STRAWBERRY GRANITA

# MENU MANAGER

THE DAY BEFORE DINNER:

1. *Make the granita.*

THE MORNING OF DINNER:

1. *Make the soup. Let cool and refrigerate.*
2. *Make the Herb-and-Lemon Yogurt and refrigerate.*

ABOUT 2 HOURS BEFORE SERVING:

1. *Roast the potatoes and set aside at room temperature.*
2. *Assemble the salmon en papillote and refrigerate.*

ABOUT 30 MINUTES BEFORE SERVING:

1. *Preheat the oven and put the salmon in the oven to bake.*
2. *Gently reheat the soup and potatoes.*

# SPRING PEA SOUP
## WITH MINT AND TOASTED PISTACHIOS

*This recipe celebrates the return of farmers' markets after winter. Make the spring-bounty soup as soon as you get home from the market, to take the pressure off the dinner hour (see Menu Manager); or, you can shell the peas for this iconic spring brew while you chat with your dinner partner. (You can also use frozen petite peas; they'll work almost as well.)* SERVES 2

¼ cup raw shelled pistachios

2 tablespoons unsalted butter

2 medium leeks, white parts only, coarsely chopped and rinsed well

3 cups chicken broth

1½ cups shelled fresh or thawed frozen green peas

¼ cup firmly packed fresh mint leaves, coarsely chopped

Salt and freshly ground black pepper

2 tablespoons crème fraîche

1. Preheat the oven to 400°F. Spread the pistachios in a pie tin and toast in the oven for 6 to 8 minutes, or until golden brown, stirring once or twice. Pour immediately onto a plate to cool. Set aside.

2. In a medium saucepan, melt the butter over medium-low heat. Add the leeks and cook, stirring often, until soft, 8 to 10 minutes.

3. Add the chicken broth and peas to the pan. Raise the heat to medium-high and bring to a boil, then reduce the heat to low and simmer, uncovered, until the peas are very tender, about 8 minutes for fresh peas or 5 minutes for frozen.

4. Remove the soup from the heat and stir in the mint. Using a hand-held blender, process the soup in the pan to a smooth purée. (Alternatively, purée in batches in a countertop blender, transferring each batch as it is finished to a bowl. Wipe the saucepan clean and return all of the puréed soup to the pan.) Season to taste with salt and pepper.

5. Just before serving, reheat the soup gently over low heat, if necessary. Ladle the soup into warmed bowls. Dollop 1 tablespoon of the crème fraîche on top of each serving and sprinkle each bowl generously with the toasted pistachios. Serve immediately.

# SALMON WITH DILL
## EN PAPILLOTE

*Salmon, with its tender, delicate yet rich meat, only gets more succulent when you semipoach-semibake the fish. That may sound funny, but it's pretty much what cooking en papillote is—which is as easy as wrapping the fillet in a parchment or foil packet with whatever flavors and accompaniments you like. Don't let yourself get tired of salmon; once you've tried this method, you may never think of panfrying or grilling it again.* SERVES 2

14 ounces salmon fillet (from the center of the fish, so it is an even thickness at both ends)

3 tablespoons unsalted butter, cut into small cubes

8 cherry tomatoes, halved lengthwise

2 or 3 thin lemon slices

2 or 3 thin orange slices

2 small bunches fresh dill, stemmed

½ cup dry white wine such as Pinot Grigio or Sauvignon Blanc

Fine sea salt and freshly ground pepper

1. Preheat the oven to 400°F.

2. Line a 6-cup glass baking dish with 2 large sheets of aluminum foil or parchment paper; the foil or parchment should extend beyond two opposite sides of the dish by 6 inches each.

3. Place the salmon, skin side down, in the dish. Scatter the butter pieces all over the fish. Add the tomato halves, cut side down, and then arrange the lemon and orange slices on top. Cover the fish with a blanket of fresh dill. Pour the white wine over the top. Season generously with salt and pepper.

4. Take up the foil or parchment flaps on the sides of the pan and bring them together, creating a loose tent over the fish. Pinch the foil or fold the paper seams together to make a snug packet that's airtight enough to hold together, but not too tight, so that steam can circulate around the fish and other ingredients while they cook. Bake for 20 to 30 minutes, or until the salmon flakes easily with a fork (after about 20 minutes, sneak open a fold to check every 3 to 4 minutes).

5. To serve, cut open the packet at the table; the escaping steam makes for a little presentation drama. Divide the fish between 2 plates and serve immediately.

# ROASTED FINGERLING POTATOES
## WITH HERB-AND-LEMON YOGURT

*Small, sweet, creamy, and a little funny to look at, these literally finger-shaped potatoes are so simple and quick to cook, they make a perfect side dish for a large crowd or just a few for two. The citrus-laced yogurt with basil is a bright and elegant twist on the traditional sour-cream-and-chive potato topper.* SERVES 2

1½ pounds small fingerling potatoes, scrubbed but not peeled

2 tablespoons olive oil

1 teaspoon minced fresh thyme

Salt and freshly ground black pepper

¾ cup whole plain yogurt

2 teaspoons minced fresh chives

2 teaspoons minced fresh basil, preferably purple

Juice of ½ lemon

1. Preheat the oven to 400°F.

2. Put the potatoes in a large bowl and drizzle with the olive oil. Add the thyme, season generously with salt and pepper, and toss until well coated.

3. Transfer the potatoes to a baking sheet and spread in a single layer, making sure that none of them are touching. (This helps the skins become crispy.)

4. Roast for 20 to 25 minutes. The potatoes should be golden and crispy brown, and a fork should easily pierce their flesh.

5. While the potatoes are roasting, in a small bowl, combine the yogurt, chives, basil, lemon juice, and salt to taste and stir to mix thoroughly.

6. Divide the potatoes between 2 dinner plates or transfer to a small shallow serving dish and serve immediately, with the yogurt on the side.

# FRESH STRAWBERRY GRANITA

*Falling somewhere between sorbets and slushies, granitas have a surprising elegance. They are pleasingly rustic and extremely easy to make—you don't even need an ice-cream maker—and for some reason the delicate icy crystals seem to enhance the flavors. This strawberry rendition is refreshing and simple; each bite tastes like a berry exploding in your mouth. This recipe actually serves 6 or more, so after a dinner for 2, be sure to eat the leftovers within a couple of days; the crystals harden into unpalatable chunks over time.* MAKES 6 CUPS

1 cup water

¾ cup sugar

2 tablespoons fresh lime juice

4 cups fresh strawberries, hulled

Small fresh mint sprigs for garnish

1. In a small saucepan over low heat, combine the water, sugar, and lime juice and cook, stirring often, until the sugar dissolves. Remove from the heat and set aside.

2. Thinly slice 1 cup of the strawberries and set aside for garnish. Put the remaining 3 cups strawberries in a food processor and process until smooth. Add the lime syrup to the strawberries and pulse until well combined.

3. Pour the strawberry mixture into a 13-by-9-by-2-inch metal baking pan. Freeze until icy around the edges, 25 to 30 minutes. Using a fork, scrape to break up the ice crystals, moving the frozen edges into the center and creating the beginnings of a granita. Return the pan to the freezer. Scrape the icy parts every 20 minutes or so, until the mixture is a uniform icy slush, 1½ to 2 hours total. Scrape the entire pan once more, then cover it tightly and freeze overnight.

4. To serve, scrape the granita into bowls and garnish each portion with the sliced strawberries and a mint sprig or two. Serve immediately.

# SPRING DINNER FOR 4

ARTICHOKE AND PARMESAN DIP

LAMB CHOPS DRIZZLED WITH MINT SABA

BABY ARUGULA WITH GRAPEFRUIT CRESCENTS AND SHAVED PARMESAN

CITRUS-BERRY-RHUBARB COMPOTE WITH HONEYED GREEK YOGURT AND TOASTED PISTACHIOS

# MENU MANAGER

UP TO 5 DAYS BEFORE DINNER:

1. *Make the compote. Let cool and refrigerate.*

THE DAY BEFORE DINNER:

1. *Make the vinaigrette and refrigerate.*

THE MORNING OF DINNER:

1. *Make the artichoke dip. Cover and refrigerate.*

ABOUT 1 HOUR BEFORE SERVING:

1. *Remove the lamb chops from the refrigerator to take the chill off, then drizzle with olive oil and sprinkle generously on both sides with salt and pepper.*
2. *Assemble and prep the ingredients for the lamb pan sauce and set aside.*

ABOUT 15 MINUTES BEFORE SERVING:

1. *Cook the lamb chops.*

JUST BEFORE SERVING DESSERT:

1. *Gently reheat the compote, if desired.*

# ARTICHOKE AND PARMESAN DIP

*This dip is a perennial and almost guaranteed crowd-pleaser. Serve it with plain crackers, slices of fresh crusty bread, crostini, even tortilla chips—any of your favorite dippers. It's also wonderful with sliced fresh vegetables such as cucumber, bell pepper, and fennel. When I have leftovers after a dinner party, I love to use it as a pasta sauce: just add a little more garlic, a splash of olive oil, and a few spoonfuls of fresh ricotta. For any course, it's absolutely divine!*

SERVES 4

1 can (14 to 16 ounces) whole artichoke hearts, drained, rinsed, and patted dry

¼ cup olive oil, plus more for garnish (optional)

1½ cups (6 ounces) freshly grated Parmesan cheese

1 to 3 garlic cloves, coarsely chopped

¼ cup chopped fresh mint, plus more for garnish (optional)

Grated zest and juice of ½ lemon, plus more zest for garnish (optional)

Sea salt

1. In a food processor, combine the artichoke hearts, olive oil, Parmesan, garlic to taste, the ¼ cup mint, and the lemon zest and juice and process to a smooth purée. Season with salt, pulsing as needed to combine. If the dip seems too thick, thin with a tablespoon or two of water.

2. Transfer the dip to a serving bowl. Garnish with a drizzle of olive oil and a bit more lemon zest and/or fresh mint, if you like.

# LAMB CHOPS
## DRIZZLED WITH MINT SABA

*These small lamb chops have always been one of my favorite foods. The bite or two of special, succulent meat on each is the perfect size, and if you love the bones, they're dainty enough to pick up and chew. Saba, a thick, syrupy grape reduction, or "must," aged in wood barrels, has been described as the original balsamic vinegar. You can find modern versions in gourmet shops and online; or substitute other good-quality balsamic vinegar syrups or aged products called "condiment" balsamics. Here, the sweet saba laced with mint is the perfect delicate accompaniment to the lamb; it enhances the flavor without ever overwhelming it.* SERVES 4

12 lamb rib chops, preferably New Zealand, each about 4 ounces and 1 inch thick

6 tablespoons olive oil

Sea salt and freshly ground black pepper

6 tablespoons unsalted butter

1 large shallot, minced

½ cup saba (see recipe introduction) or excellent-quality condiment or aged (preferably at least 12 years) balsamic vinegar

½ cup minced fresh mint

1. Bring the lamb chops to room temperature. Rub the chops on all sides with 4 tablespoons of the olive oil, then season generously with salt and pepper.

2. In a large skillet over medium-high heat, heat the remaining 2 tablespoons olive oil until smoking. Add the lamb chops and cook, turning once, until nicely browned on both sides and cooked to the desired doneness, about 3 minutes per side for rare, 4 minutes per side for medium-rare. Transfer to a platter and let rest.

3. Meanwhile, in a small saucepan, melt the butter over medium heat. Add the shallot and sauté until translucent, about 5 minutes. Add the saba and stir until well combined. Cook until the mixture is bubbly and fragrant, about 3 minutes. The sauce should be syrupy. Remove from the heat, cover to keep warm, and set aside.

4. To serve, arrange 3 chops on each of 4 plates. Stir the mint into the warm saba, drizzle over the chops, and serve immediately.

# BABY ARUGULA
## WITH GRAPEFRUIT CRESCENTS AND SHAVED PARMESAN

*The bright herbal dressing here helps cut the richness of meat, making this salad a great accompaniment to dishes like the lamb chops on the menu (page 26). The fresh, earthy flavors are delicious on any number of salads, so cover and refridgerate the remaining vinaigrette for up to 2 weeks.* SERVES 4

FRESH HERBAL VINAIGRETTE

1 garlic clove, minced

1½ teaspoons Dijon mustard

Pinch of sugar

1½ teaspoons minced fresh thyme

1 teaspoon *each* minced fresh oregano, basil, and mint

1 tablespoon Champagne vinegar

1½ teaspoons fresh lemon juice

¾ cup extra-virgin olive oil

Sea salt and freshly ground black pepper

4 cups (about 4 ounces) baby arugula

½ small ruby red grapefruit, peeled

1 cup (4 ounces) shaved Parmesan cheese

1. To make the vinaigrette, in a small bowl, whisk together the garlic, Dijon, sugar, thyme, oregano, basil, mint, vinegar, and lemon juice. Slowly pour in the olive oil, whisking constantly until the dressing is well blended and creamy. Season with salt and pepper.

2. Put the arugula in a salad bowl. Cut the grapefruit into disks, then cut each slice in half. Place the grapefruit pieces on top of the arugula, then toss in as much of the dressing as you like, adding it a tablespoon or so at a time and tossing in between to avoid overdressing. Three to 5 tablespoons should be enough. (Store any remaining vinaigrette, tightly covered in the refrigerator, for up to 1 month.) Sprinkle the Parmesan shavings on top and serve immediately.

# CITRUS-BERRY-RHUBARB COMPOTE
## WITH HONEYED GREEK YOGURT AND TOASTED PISTACHIOS

*This recipe is so-so-so: so simple, so delicious, and so quick. I like to serve it with rich, whole-fat Greek yogurt and toasted pistachios, but you can certainly make it with any style yogurt, or crème fraîche or vanilla ice cream, for that matter, and/or change up the nuts with toasted walnuts or toasted almonds.* SERVES 4

½ cup raw shelled pistachios

COMPOTE

Grated zest of 2 clementines

Juice of 6 clementines

1½ cups sugar

2 cups water

4 medium stalks rhubarb (about 1 pound total), cut into 1-inch pieces

2 cups fresh strawberries, hulled

1. Preheat the oven to 400°F.

2. Spread the pistachios in a pie tin and toast in the oven for 6 to 8 minutes, or until golden brown, stirring once or twice. Pour immediately onto a plate to cool. Chop coarsely and set aside.

3. To make the compote, in a large saucepan over medium-high heat, stir together the clementine zest and juice, sugar, and water and bring to a boil, stirring to dissolve the sugar. Reduce the heat to medium-low and let the mixture simmer until slightly thickened, about 3 minutes. Add the rhubarb, return to a simmer, and cook until the rhubarb is tender when pierced with a fork, about 20 minutes. Add the strawberries, reduce the heat to low, and continue to simmer until the fruit is broken down and the juices have thickened, about 40 minutes longer, stirring occasionally to make sure the bottom doesn't scorch. The consistency of the compote should be a little looser than jam. Remove from the heat and cover to keep warm. (If preparing ahead of time, let cool, cover tightly, and refrigerate for up to 5 days. Bring to room temperature or reheat gently before serving.)

HONEYED GREEK YOGURT

2 cups whole plain Greek yogurt

3 tablespoons wildflower honey

1 vanilla bean, split lengthwise

4. To make the honeyed yogurt, in a bowl, whisk together the yogurt and honey. Using the tip of a small, sharp knife, scrape the seeds from the vanilla bean into the yogurt mixture and stir to mix well. Discard the bean pod (or reserve for another use).

5. To serve, divide the yogurt among 4 bowls. Scoop the compote over the top of each portion, dividing it evenly, and sprinkle generously with the toasted pistachios. Serve immediately.

# SPRING DINNER FOR 6

TANGY, PEPPERY WATERCRESS SOUP

PORK ROAST WITH MUSTARD-AND-HERB CRUST

ENDIVE SALAD WITH MANGO, AVOCADO, AND RED ONION

PISTACHIO-CARDAMOM CAKE WITH LIME SYRUP

# MENU MANAGER

THE DAY BEFORE DINNER:

1. *Make the soup. Let cool and refrigerate.*

THE MORNING OF DINNER:

1. *Make the vinaigrette and refrigerate.*
2. *Make the cake and set aside at room temperature.*

ABOUT 3 HOURS BEFORE SERVING:

1. *Bring the meat to room temperature.*
2. *Make the mustard-and-herb mixture for the pork.*

ABOUT 2 HOURS BEFORE SERVING:

1. *Rub the mustard-and-herb mixture on the pork roast and put the roast in the oven.*
2. *Prepare the ingredients for the salad, except for the avocados, and refrigerate.*

ABOUT 40 MINUTES BEFORE SERVING:

1. *Remove the vinaigrette from the fridge to bring it to room temperature.*

JUST BEFORE SERVING:

1. *Gently reheat the soup and whip the cream for the garnish.*
2. *Prepare the avocados; assemble and dress the salad.*

# TANGY, PEPPERY WATERCRESS SOUP

*My mother made this soup often, and always raved about how delicious it was. So I finally had to make it for myself to see—and she was right! The slightly peppery taste of the watercress is mellowed by the potatoes and brightened by the lemon. This smooth, tasty soup is a perfect starter; or for a quieter, less ambitious evening, it is wonderful served as a meal in itself with a loaf of heated bread and butter.* SERVES 6

Sea salt and freshly ground black pepper

2 pounds watercress, stemmed

2 tablespoons unsalted butter

1 medium yellow onion, chopped

8 cups chicken broth

2 medium russet potatoes, peeled and cut into ½-inch dice

2 to 3 tablespoons fresh lemon juice

½ cup heavy (whipping) cream

¼ cup minced fresh chives

1. Bring a pot of salted water to a boil over high heat. Meanwhile, prepare a large bowl of ice water.

2. Plunge the watercress into the boiling water and cook for about 2 minutes, or until wilted and bright green. Drain and immediately submerge in the ice water to stop the cooking. Drain again thoroughly. Chop coarsely and set aside.

3. Melt the butter in a large saucepan over medium heat. Add the onion and cook, stirring often, until translucent, 8 to 10 minutes. Add the chicken broth and potatoes. Raise the heat to medium-high and bring to a boil. Reduce the heat to medium and simmer, stirring occasionally, until the potatoes are tender, about 20 minutes. Remove from the heat.

4. Add the chopped watercress to the soup. Using a hand-held blender, process the soup in the pan to a smooth purée. (Alternatively, purée in batches in a countertop blender, transferring each batch as it is finished to a bowl. Wipe the saucepan clean and return all of the puréed soup to the pan.) Stir in the lemon juice. Season to taste with salt and pepper. (If preparing ahead of time, cover and refrigerate.)

5. Just before serving, gently reheat the soup, if necessary. Meanwhile, in a large bowl, combine the cream and a pinch of salt and whisk or beat using an electric mixer until soft peaks form. Fold in about half of the chives.

6. Ladle the soup into warmed bowls and top each with a dollop of the chive whipped cream. Garnish with the remaining chives and serve immediately.

# PORK ROAST
## WITH MUSTARD-AND-HERB CRUST

*Roasts are wonderful for a group because they take little effort to produce divine results. You just have to be sure not to overcook them—that's the only thing that can go really wrong when preparing a roast, be it pork, poultry, or beef. You'll love the crust on this succulent cut of pork. It adds both flavor and texture to the delicious, slow-cooked meat.*

SERVES 6

1 boneless pork loin roast (3 to 4 pounds), skin removed but with a good layer of surrounding fat

¼ cup olive oil

3 tablespoons Dijon mustard

4 garlic cloves, coarsely chopped

¼ cup chopped fresh thyme

¼ cup chopped fresh rosemary

2 tablespoons chopped fresh oregano

1½ teaspoons sea salt

1 teaspoon freshly ground black pepper

½ cup dried bread crumbs

1. Remove the roast from the refrigerator 1 hour before roasting. Preheat the oven to 350°F. Line a roasting pan with aluminum foil and place a rack in the pan.

2. In a bowl, combine the olive oil, mustard, garlic, thyme, rosemary, oregano, salt, and pepper and stir to mix well. Add the bread crumbs and stir until thoroughly blended.

3. Put the pork roast on the rack, fat side up. Spread the mustard-herb mixture all over the roast and place it in the oven. Roast until an instant-read thermometer inserted into the thickest part registers 145°F, 1 to 1½ hours.

4. Transfer the roast to a cutting board and let rest for about 10 minutes. Carve across the grain on the diagonal into thin slices and serve immediately.

# ENDIVE SALAD
## WITH MANGO, AVOCADO, AND RED ONION

*Tender, firm, bitter, sweet, and creamy with a nice big crunch, this salad has it all. It's perfect with meat or fish, especially pork, lamb, or salmon. If a perfectly ripe mango is not available, you can substitute an orange—or even better, a blood orange.* SERVES 6

CHAMPAGNE VINAIGRETTE

4 teaspoons Champagne vinegar

1 teaspoon fresh lemon juice

1 shallot, minced

2 teaspoons Dijon mustard

¼ teaspoon sugar

¾ cup extra-virgin olive oil

Sea salt and freshly ground black pepper

8 endives, quartered, cored, and coarsely chopped

1 large ripe mango, halved, peeled, and cut into 1-inch strips

2 ripe avocados, halved, pitted, peeled, and thinly sliced

½ medium red onion, thinly sliced

1. To make the vinaigrette, in a bowl, whisk together the vinegar, lemon juice, shallot, mustard, and sugar. Slowly pour in the olive oil, whisking constantly until the dressing is well blended. Season with salt and pepper.

2. In a salad bowl, combine the endives, mango, avocados, and onion and toss gently to distribute. Just before serving, add about half of the vinaigrette and toss gently to coat. Add more vinaigrette a little at a time just to coat, if needed. (Store any remaining vinaigrette tightly covered in the refrigerator for up to 1 month.) Serve immediately.

# PISTACHIO-CARDAMOM CAKE
## WITH LIME SYRUP

*This syrup is divine. I like to double the amount of syrup. Of course, some may like less, but I'm someone who likes the nutty cake drenched in the tart, gooey syrup.* MAKES ONE 8-INCH ROUND CAKE; SERVES 6 TO 8

Butter for greasing, plus 10 tablespoons unsalted butter, at room temperature

1 cup raw shelled pistachios

1 teaspoon ground cardamom

1 tablespoon unbleached all-purpose flour, plus 1½ cups

1¾ cups sugar

1¾ teaspoons baking powder

⅓ teaspoon salt

3 large eggs

½ cup whole plain yogurt

LIME SYRUP

½ cup fresh lime juice

Zest of 1 lime

¾ cup sugar

1. Preheat the oven to 350°F. Lightly butter an 8-inch round cake pan.

2. In a food processor, combine the pistachios, the cardamom, and the 1 tablespoon flour and pulse just until finely ground. (Be careful not to over grind or you may get nut butter.)

3. In a large bowl, whisk together the ground pistachio mixture, ¾ cup of the sugar, the 1½ cups flour, the baking powder, and the salt. Add the 10 tablespoons butter in small pieces, toss to distribute, and stir just until combined.

4. In a small bowl, whisk together the eggs and yogurt. Fold the egg mixture into the dry ingredients with a rubber spatula until well combined. Spread the batter evenly in the prepared pan.

5. Bake for 50 minutes, or until a knife inserted into the center comes out clean. Transfer to a wire rack and let cool for about 15 minutes. Invert the pan and unmold the cake onto another rack. Let cool for another 20 to 30 minutes.

*continued* >

6. Meanwhile make the lime syrup: In a small saucepan, combine the lime zest and juice and the sugar and bring to a boil over medium-high heat. Reduce the heat to medium-low and simmer for 5 minutes, stirring to help dissolve the sugar. Set aside for 15 minutes to allow the syrup to thicken and get infused with the lime.

7. Poke the cake all over with a long wooden skewer while it is still slightly warm. Drizzle the syrup all over the cake and let it soak in. Be sure to use all of the syrup; the more syrup, the better. Cut into wedges and serve.

# SUMMER

# SUMMER DINNER FOR 2

MARINATED OLIVES

MUSSELS WITH WHITE WINE, FENNEL, AND LEEKS

RAW CORN SALAD WITH CILANTRO, LIME, AND JALAPEÑO

FRESH CHERRIES WITH BITTERSWEET CHOCOLATE SAUCE

# MENU MANAGER

2 OR 3 DAYS BEFORE DINNER:

1. *Marinate the olives.*

ABOUT 3 HOURS BEFORE SERVING:

1. *Make the corn salad and refrigerate.*
2. *Make the chocolate dipping sauce and set aside at room temperature.*
3. *Scrub and debeard the mussels and store on ice in the refrigerator.*

ABOUT 1 HOUR BEFORE SERVING:

1. *Remove the corn salad from the fridge to bring it to room temperature.*
2. *Prepare the vegetables for the mussels and refrigerate.*

JUST BEFORE SERVING:

1. *Cook the mussels.*

JUST BEFORE SERVING DESSERT:

1. *Gently reheat the chocolate sauce.*

# MARINATED OLIVES

*These olives should be made a couple of days ahead so that the flavors of the marinade can penetrate the flesh. You'll have more olives than you need to serve two, but they will keep beautifully in an airtight container in the refrigerator for up to a couple of months. I love to eat them as a snack with wine and/or a nutty, hard cheese and crackers.* MAKES 2 CUPS

1 cup picholine olives

1 cup niçoise olives

1 garlic clove, lightly crushed

Leaves of 2 large fresh rosemary sprigs

½ lemon, thinly sliced

½ cup olive oil

1. Drain the olives and put them in a container with a tight-fitting lid. Add the garlic, rosemary leaves, lemon slices, and olive oil. Put the cover on the container and shake a few times to mix well. Let sit at room temperature for about 2 hours.

2. Shake the container again thoroughly and transfer to the refrigerator. The olives will keep, tightly covered in the refrigerator, for up to 2 months. Bring to room temperature before serving.

# MUSSELS

## WITH WHITE WINE, FENNEL, AND LEEKS

*This simple spin on the French preparation for mussels is delicious and quick. The plump, juicy mussels are enhanced by the earthy-sweet taste of the leeks and the distinctive fresh taste of fennel. Serve with a good, warm fresh baguette and you've got a perfect meal.* SERVES 2

1 tablespoon unsalted butter

2 tablespoons olive oil

2 medium leeks, white and tender green parts only, thinly sliced and rinsed well

1 medium fennel bulb, trimmed, quartered, cored, and thinly sliced

1 garlic clove, coarsely chopped

1 teaspoon fresh thyme leaves

3 pounds fresh mussels, scrubbed and debearded

1 cup dry white wine such as Sauvignon Blanc

Salt and freshly ground black pepper

¼ cup chopped fresh flat-leaf (Italian) parsley

1. In a stockpot or large saucepan over medium heat, melt the butter in the olive oil until the butter is melted and the fats are sizzling. Add the leeks, fennel, garlic, and thyme and cook until the vegetables are translucent and soft, 5 to 7 minutes.

2. Add the mussels to the pot, discarding any that do not close to the touch, and toss with the vegetable mixture.

3. Pour in the wine and season generously with salt and pepper. Cover and steam for about 8 minutes, shaking the covered pot once or twice. Uncover the pot and peek; if some of the mussels have not opened yet, give them about 2 minutes more.

4. Divide the mussels between 2 large plates or individual shallow bowls, discarding any that failed to open. Garnish with the parsley and serve immediately.

# RAW CORN SALAD
## WITH CILANTRO, LIME, AND JALAPEÑO

*This salad is colorful and flavorful; the aromatics, citrus, herbs, and spices all meld together beautifully. Although it might seem strange to serve a raw corn salad with mussels, the fresh kernels are sweet and clean tasting against the rich mussel broth. Perhaps best of all, it's a crowd-pleasing vegetable side dish that can be made without ever turning on the oven in hot weather. This summer salad is great in its classic role alongside grilled chicken or steak, too.* SERVES 2

3 large ears of corn, shucked

3 tablespoons coarsely chopped roasted red pepper

1 small red bell pepper, halved, seeded, and coarsely chopped

2 tablespoons minced red onion

3 tablespoons minced fresh cilantro

1 small jalapeño chile, seeds and white ribs and membranes removed, minced

Juice of 2 or 3 limes

2 tablespoons olive oil

Sea salt and freshly ground black pepper

1. Remove the corn kernels from the cobs: Working with one at a time, hold an ear of corn upright in a large, shallow bowl. Using a sharp chef's knife, cut down along the ear, following the contours and being sure to keep the edge of the blade pressed against the cob to extract all of the sweet juices.

2. Add the roasted red pepper, fresh red pepper, onion, cilantro, and about half of the jalapeño to the bowl with the corn and stir well to combine. Add the juice of 2 limes, the olive oil, and salt and pepper to taste. Taste and add more lime juice if the mixture seems to need extra tang and more jalapeño if you want more heat. Serve immediately, or cover and refrigerate for up to a week. Bring to room temperature before serving.

# FRESH CHERRIES
## WITH BITTERSWEET CHOCOLATE SAUCE

*What's more deliciously simple than fresh fruit with homemade chocolate dipping sauce? Not much! For this presentation, I suggest 1 to 2 pounds of cherries, which may seem like a lot—but trust me, this dessert is addicting. You won't want to stop dipping them and dropping them into your mouth, so better to have too much than too little.* SERVES 2

BITTERSWEET CHOCOLATE SAUCE

4 ounces bittersweet chocolate, coarsely chopped

3 tablespoons unsalted butter, at room temperature

⅔ cup water

2 tablespoons sugar

3 tablespoons corn syrup

3 tablespoons heavy (whipping) cream

Pinch of salt

1 to 2 pounds fresh cherries

1. To make the chocolate sauce, in a medium heatproof bowl, combine the chocolate and butter. Set aside.

2. In a medium saucepan, combine the water, sugar, corn syrup, cream, and salt. Bring to a rolling boil over high heat, stirring occasionally to dissolve the sugar. When the sugar is dissolved and the mixture is boiling, immediately pour over the chocolate and butter. Let sit undisturbed for 2 minutes, then whisk the sauce until fully combined.

3. Scrape the chocolate sauce into the saucepan you made the syrup mixture in and bring to a simmer over medium-low heat. Simmer for 5 to 10 minutes, stirring constantly, until the sauce thickens enough to coat the back of the spoon. Immediately remove from the heat. If the sauce separates or appears greasy at any point, remove it from the heat and whisk in a couple drops of hot water to bring it back together. Set aside until ready to serve.

4. Just before serving, gently reheat the sauce and transfer to a serving bowl or individual dipping bowls. Put the cherries in a large bowl or smaller individual bowls and serve immediately, with the dipping sauce alongside. (Store any remaining sauce, tightly covered in the refrigerator, for up to 1 week.)

# SUMMER DINNER FOR 4

WATERMELON COOLERS WITH FRESH MINT

ROASTED ALMONDS WITH SEA SALT AND ROSEMARY

CHILLED CUCUMBER SOUP WITH DILL

HOMEY HERBED TOMATO TART WITH CARAMELIZED LEEKS

CRISPY HEARTS OF ROMAINE WITH LEMON VINAIGRETTE

PERFECTLY ROSY PEACHES WITH CRÈME FRAÎCHE

# MENU MANAGER

UP TO 2 WEEKS BEFORE DINNER:

1. *Make the roasted almonds. Let cool and store in an airtight container at room temperature.*

THE DAY BEFORE DINNER:

1. *Make the soup and refrigerate.*
2. *Cube and freeze the watermelon for the coolers.*
3. *Make the dough for the tomato tart crust and refrigerate.*

THE MORNING OF DINNER:

1. *Make the lemon vinaigrette and refrigerate.*
2. *Poach the peaches, if making ahead, and refrigerate in their poaching liquid.*

ABOUT 2 HOURS BEFORE SERVING:

1. *Wash and thoroughly dry the romaine hearts; refrigerate.*
2. *Bring the dough to room temperature while you preheat the oven; assemble and bake the tart.*
3. *Finish the syrup for the peaches; set the syrup and peaches aside separately at room temperature.*

ABOUT 30 MINUTES BEFORE SERVING:

1. *Remove the vinaigrette from the fridge to bring it to room temperature.*

JUST BEFORE YOUR GUESTS ARRIVE:

1. *Put the nuts in small serving bowls.*
2. *Blend the watermelon coolers.*

# WATERMELON COOLERS
## WITH FRESH MINT

*There are three important qualities in a summer libation: refreshing, refreshing, and refreshing. You can add a shot of vodka to these coolers to give them a kick, or just enjoy the sweet, clean, summery taste of watermelon, lime, and mint.* SERVES 4

One 3-pound seedless watermelon, peeled, cubed, and frozen

1 cup club soda

4 ounces vodka (optional)

¼ cup fresh lime juice

2 tablespoons coarsely chopped fresh mint, plus 4 small sprigs for garnish

8 to 10 ice cubes

½ lime, cut into 4 thin rounds

1. In a blender, combine the frozen watermelon, club soda, vodka (if using), lime juice, chopped mint, and ice cubes and blend until smooth.

2. Divide the watermelon mixture among 4 wineglasses. Garnish each cooler with a mint sprig and a lime slice and serve immediately.

# ROASTED ALMONDS
## WITH SEA SALT AND ROSEMARY

*I love these nuts! They taste better than any roasted variety I've ever picked up in a store—no matter how fresh. The addition of fresh rosemary draws out the almonds' buttery flavor. Store leftovers in an airtight container at room temperature for up to 2 weeks.* MAKES 4 CUPS

4 cups raw whole almonds

3 tablespoons olive oil

1½ tablespoons minced fresh rosemary

1 teaspoon fleur de sel or coarse sea salt

1. Preheat the oven to 375°F.

2. In a large bowl, combine the almonds, olive oil, rosemary, and salt and stir until the almonds are evenly coated.

3. Spread the almonds in a single layer on 1 large or 2 small rimmed baking sheets. Roast, stirring once or twice, until fragrant and toasted, 5 to 7 minutes. Remove from the oven and let cool on the pan(s) for about 3 minutes, then transfer to paper towels to drain and cool completely.

# CHILLED CUCUMBER SOUP
## WITH DILL

*This tangy, earthy, and gorgeous pale green cold soup is the perfect foil to a hot day. It goes beautifully with everything in this mellow summer menu, but call upon it all summer long for lunches or light dinners with nothing more than a loaf of warm, dark bread. Make sure you refrigerate the soup for at least 3 hours before serving. I recommend making it the day before; that way the soup is sure to be well chilled, and the flavors will deepen, too.* SERVES 4

3 large cucumbers (about 2 pounds total), peeled, seeded, and coarsely chopped

¼ red onion, coarsely chopped

3 or 4 large garlic cloves, coarsely chopped

1½ tablespoons olive oil

¼ loaf day-old French bread, crust removed, coarsely chopped

4 cups whole plain Greek yogurt

1 tablespoon fresh lemon juice or Champagne vinegar, or more if needed

Salt and freshly ground black pepper

¼ cup minced fresh dill

1. In a blender, combine the cucumbers, onion, garlic, olive oil, bread, and yogurt and blend until smooth.

2. Add the lemon juice and pulse just to combine. Season with salt and pepper. Taste and add more lemon juice, if needed. Transfer to an airtight container or cover in the blender and refrigerate until well chilled, at least 3 hours or preferably overnight. (The soup may be refrigerated for up to 1 week.)

3. When you are ready to serve, whisk or blend the soup again lightly. Divide among 4 chilled bowls, garnish with the dill, and serve immediately.

# CRISPY HEARTS OF ROMAINE
## WITH LEMON VINAIGRETTE

*I find this simple salad to be a perfect contrast to the sweet, juicy, savory tomato tart (page 59). It's crisp, clean, and super crunchy. You can buy romaine hearts in bags already prepared, but it's easy enough (and more economical) to buy whole heads of lettuce. Just peel off a few layers of the large, dark green outer leaves to reveal the tender, light green hearts. Use the rest of the leaves for a salad the next night.* SERVES 4

LEMON VINAIGRETTE

1½ tablespoons fresh lemon juice

1 tablespoon Dijon mustard

¾ teaspoon honey

¼ cup extra-virgin olive oil

Salt and freshly ground black pepper

2 hearts of romaine lettuce, halved lengthwise

1. To make the vinaigrette, in a small bowl, whisk together the lemon juice, mustard, and honey. Slowly pour in the olive oil, whisking constantly until the dressing is well mixed and creamy. Season with salt and pepper.

2. Put the halved romaine hearts in a salad bowl, drizzle in the lemon vinaigrette, and toss gently to coat. Serve immediately.

SABATIER

# HOMEY HERBED TOMATO TART
## WITH CARAMELIZED LEEKS

*This perfect summer tart is easy, simple and so, so good! You can make it for you and a friend or a couple for a large group. It's one of those dishes you'll make over and over again. Create your own variations on the herbed crust using different fresh herbs, and try other toppings depending on the season.* MAKES ONE 9- OR 10-INCH TART; SERVES 4

HERB CRUST

1½ teaspoons instant active dry yeast

½ teaspoon honey

½ cup warm water (105° to 115°F)

3 tablespoons extra-virgin olive oil, plus more for brushing

1 large egg

2 teaspoons chopped fresh flat-leaf (Italian) parsley

1 teaspoon chopped fresh chives

2 cups unbleached all-purpose flour

¾ teaspoon fine sea salt

1. To make the crust, in the bowl of a stand mixer fitted with the dough hook, combine the yeast, honey, warm water, the 3 tablespoons olive oil, the egg, parsley, chives, and 1¾ cups of the flour. Stir gently a few times with a spoon, then add the salt. Turn the mixer on low and beat gently until the flour is completely moistened, about 1 minute. Raise the speed to medium-low and beat until the dough is smooth and elastic, about 5 minutes. If the dough seems very sticky, beat in the remaining ¼ cup flour. (Alternatively, combine the ingredients in a large bowl, adding the flour in parts as directed. Beat with a wooden spoon until well combined, then turn out onto a lightly floured work surface and knead until a smooth, elastic dough forms, about 10 minutes.)

2. Transfer the dough to a large oiled bowl and turn to coat. Cover loosely with a damp kitchen towel or plastic wrap and let rise in a warm place until doubled in bulk, about 45 minutes.

3. Turn the dough out onto a large oiled plate. Press out the air and shape into a disk. Cover with plastic wrap and refrigerate for at least 8 hours or up to overnight.

*continued >*

FILLING

3 tablespoons unsalted butter

2 large leeks, white and tender green parts only, thinly sliced and rinsed well

2 garlic cloves, crushed

1 teaspoon minced fresh basil

1 teaspoon minced fresh oregano

4 large ripe tomatoes, preferably heirloom, cut into slices a scant ½ inch thick

8 golden cherry tomatoes, halved

1 tablespoon olive oil, plus more for brushing

¼ cup pitted niçoise olives, coarsely chopped

5 tablespoons freshly grated Parmesan cheese

4. Bring the dough back to room temperature, then lightly brush a 9- or 10-inch tart pan or pie plate with olive oil. Set aside.

5. Unwrap the dough disk and place on a lightly floured work surface. Roll out into a round about 16 inches in diameter. Gently lift the dough round and place it in the prepared pan, pressing it to fit into the bottom and sides. Trim the excess dough to about 1 inch of overhang, then fold and pinch all around the edge to make a pretty crimped border. Return to the refrigerator until the filling is ready. Preheat the oven to 400°F.

6. To make the filling, in a sauté pan or skillet over medium heat, melt the butter. Add the leeks and sauté for 10 minutes. When they start to become translucent and soft, add the garlic and sauté for another 5 minutes. When the leeks are very soft, almost mushy, remove from the heat. Stir in the basil and oregano.

7. Spread the leek mixture evenly over the bottom of the crust. Carefully arrange the tomato slices in concentric circles on top, starting at the outside edge and working toward the center, overlapping them slightly if necessary. Arrange the cherry tomato halves, cut side up, over the tomato slices. Drizzle with the 1 tablespoon olive oil. Sprinkle the olives evenly over all, then the Parmesan.

8. Bake the tart until the crust is golden on the edges, the tomatoes are soft and gooey, and the juices are bubbling, 35 to 45 minutes. Brush the crust with a little more olive oil as soon as you take the tart out of the oven. Let cool slightly, then cut into wedges and serve.

# PERFECTLY ROSY PEACHES
## WITH CRÈME FRAÎCHE

*These peaches, as you may guess, are delicious with ice cream—especially, I think, vanilla, strawberry, or ginger. They're also delicious spooned over oatmeal or with yogurt for breakfast. They are so versatile, in fact, it's worth doubling or tripling the recipe when peaches are in season; keep some in the refrigerator for a snack, breakfast, or dessert all week. The ingredients list is flexible, too: you can use white peaches, yellow peaches, nectarines, or plums. Just be sure they're in season and ripe.* SERVES 4

2 cups dry rosé wine

½ cup sugar

2 strips orange zest, about ½ inch wide and 3 inches long

2 fresh rosemary sprigs

1¼ cups water

4 ripe yellow or white peaches or nectarines (about 1¼ pounds total), quartered and pitted

¼ to ½ cup crème fraîche

1. In a saucepan over medium heat, combine the wine, sugar, orange zest, rosemary, and water and bring to a simmer, stirring to dissolve the sugar. Add the peaches, skin side down, and simmer for 15 minutes, or until soft. Remove from the heat and let the peaches cool to room temperature in the poaching liquid. (You can cover and refrigerate the peaches in their liquid at this point for up to 1 day.)

2. Using a slotted spoon, transfer the peaches carefully to a wide bowl, placing them in a single layer.

3. Return the poaching liquid to medium heat and return to a simmer. Cook until reduced to a slightly syrupy texture (but not as thick as chocolate syrup; you want it to remain somewhat runny), 20 to 30 minutes longer. Remove from the heat. Discard the rosemary sprigs and orange zest.

4. To serve, place 4 peach quarters, flesh side up, in each of 4 dessert dishes. Drizzle each portion generously with the rosé syrup and top with 1 to 2 tablespoons of the crème fraîche. Serve immediately. (Store any remaining rosé syrup in a tightly sealed jar in the refrigerator for up to 1 month.)

# SUMMER DINNER FOR 6

SPICY GINGER-MINT COCKTAILS

ROAST CHICKEN STUFFED WITH LEMON AND ROSEMARY

QUINOA SALAD WITH RADICCHIO, NECTARINES, AND
CITRUS-CHAMPAGNE VINAIGRETTE

RAW SUMMER SQUASH SALAD WITH FRENCH FETA AND TOASTED PINE NUTS

PLUM-BLACKBERRY-PEACH CRISP WITH VANILLA ICE CREAM
WITH A DASH OF CINNAMON

# MENU MANAGER

UP TO 3 DAYS BEFORE DINNER:

1. *Make the ice cream.*

THE MORNING OF DINNER:

1. *Make the crisp and set aside at room temperature.*
2. *Make the two vinaigrettes for the salads and refrigerate.*

ABOUT 3 HOURS BEFORE SERVING:

1. *Make the quinoa salad; refrigerate without dressing.*
2. *Prepare the chicken for roasting and refrigerate.*
3. *Prepare the squash for the salad and refrigerate; toast the pine nuts.*

ABOUT 1½ HOURS BEFORE SERVING:

1. *Remove the chicken from the fridge to take the chill off while you preheat the oven, then roast the chicken.*
2. *Remove the quinoa salad and the two vinaigrettes from the fridge to bring to room temperature.*

JUST BEFORE SERVING:

1. *Dress the quinoa salad.*
2. *Assemble and dress the squash salad.*

JUST BEFORE SERVING DESSERT:

1. *Gently rewarm the crisp, if desired.*

# SPICY GINGER-MINT COCKTAILS

*Try this cocktail and it may well become the easy go-to drink in your house. Now that there are so many great-quality "real" ginger ales for sale, you can be choosey about your favorite. Some have much more spice than others; I prefer the spiciest.* SERVES 6

Ice cubes

9 ounces vodka

Four 12-ounce bottles artisanal ginger ale

12 small fresh mint sprigs

1 lime, cut into 6 thin rounds

1. Fill four 2-cup glasses with ice. Add 1½ ounces vodka to each glass and pour in ginger ale to fill.

2. Garnish each glass with 2 sprigs of mint and a lime slice and serve.

# ROAST CHICKEN
## STUFFED WITH LEMON AND ROSEMARY

*This chicken is wonderful both hot out of the oven and at room temperature, leaving you flexible for how you want to serve your guests. It's also so simple, you can put it in the oven right before your guests arrive and have plenty of time to sip your Spicy Ginger-Mint Cocktails (page 67) with them while it cooks. The rosemary imparts a nice buttery flavor, while the lemon adds the citrus accent that goes so beautifully with poultry.* SERVES 6

2 chickens (about 3 pounds each)

Sea salt

3 lemons, quartered

14 or 16 fresh rosemary sprigs, each about 3 inches long

¼ cup olive oil

1. Preheat the oven to 425°F.

2. Remove the necks and giblets from the chickens and reserve for another use. Rinse the chickens inside and out and pat dry with paper towels. Salt the body cavities liberally and stuff 6 lemon quarters into each. Gently separating the skin from the flesh with your fingers, insert 7 or 8 rosemary sprigs under the skin of each bird. Slide the sprigs in lengthwise and distribute them evenly all around the breasts and thighs. Rub the skin with olive oil. Tie the drumsticks together at the ankles with kitchen twine. Salt the skin just before placing the prepared birds in the roasting pan.

3. Place the chickens, breast side up, on a large rack in a large roasting pan. Roast until an instant-read thermometer inserted into the thickest part of a thigh but not touching the bone registers 170°F, or until the juices run clear from the thickest part of the thigh when pierced with a fork, about 1 hour.

4. Remove the chickens from the oven. Transfer to a cutting board and let rest for 10 minutes, then carve across the grain on the diagonal into thin slices and serve.

# RAW SUMMER SQUASH SALAD
## WITH FRENCH FETA AND TOASTED PINE NUTS

*If truth must be told, I am not a big fan of zucchini or yellow squash. But when either of them is sliced paper-thin or shaved into ribbons, I feel very differently—I actually really like them. This is the salad that changed my mind; a mix of both seasonal favorites creates a pretty bowl of color.* SERVES 6

3 tablespoons pine nuts

1½ pounds mixed baby zucchini and yellow squash

Salt

CITRONETTE

½ teaspoon finely grated lemon zest

1 tablespoon fresh lemon juice

1 large garlic clove, minced

1 teaspoon chopped fresh thyme

1 teaspoon chopped fresh tarragon

1 teaspoon chopped fresh flat-leaf (Italian) parsley

3 tablespoons olive oil

1 cup French feta cheese, crumbled

1. Preheat the oven to 375°F. Spread the pine nuts in a pie tin and toast in the oven for 5 to 7 minutes, or until lightly browned, stirring once or twice. Pour immediately onto a plate to cool. Set aside.

2. Using a cheese slicer, a mandoline, or a vegetable peeler, carefully shave the squashes into paper-thin ribbons. Discard the cores when they get too seedy. Spread the ribbons on a cutting board and sprinkle them liberally with salt. Let sit for 20 minutes.

3. Rinse the squash well and gently pat them dry. Place in a serving bowl and refrigerate until ready to serve.

4. To make the citronette, in a small bowl, whisk together the lemon zest and juice, garlic, thyme, tarragon, and parsley. Slowly drizzle in the olive oil, whisking constantly until the dressing is well blended. Set aside until ready to serve.

5. Right before serving, whisk the citronette again. Combine the feta, squash, and citronette in a large salad bowl and toss to mix and coat well. Serve immediately.

# QUINOA SALAD WITH RADICCHIO,
## NECTARINES, AND CITRUS-CHAMPAGNE VINAIGRETTE

*This salad is healthy, summery, pretty to look at—and yes, delicious to eat. I like to use white nectarines for this mix, as they are the sweetest in the nectarine family and also often a little crunchier than their orange cousins. Transform this summer version to one for winter by substituting blood oranges for the white nectarines.* SERVES 6

CITRUS-CHAMPAGNE VINAIGRETTE

1 tablespoon Champagne vinegar

1 tablespoon fresh lemon juice

2 teaspoons finely grated orange zest

Salt and freshly ground black pepper

⅓ cup extra-virgin olive oil

1 large head radicchio, cored and chopped (about 3 cups)

1 cup quinoa, cooked according to the package directions and cooled to room temperature

3 white nectarines, pitted and cut into ¼-inch slices

2 tablespoons minced fresh mint

1. To make the vinaigrette, in a small bowl, whisk together the vinegar, lemon juice, orange zest, and a pinch each of salt and pepper. Slowly pour in the olive oil, whisking constantly until the dressing is well blended and creamy. Taste and adjust the seasoning. Set aside.

2. In a salad bowl, combine the radicchio, cooled quinoa, nectarines, and mint and toss gently to distribute the ingredients. (Serve right away, or cover and refrigerate for up to 2 hours. Return to room temperature before serving.)

3. Immediately before serving, drizzle the salad with the Citrus-Champagne Vinaigrette and toss gently to coat.

# PLUM-BLACKBERRY-PEACH CRISP
## WITH VANILLA ICE CREAM WITH A DASH OF CINNAMON

*When I make a crisp, if it doesn't get completely eaten the night I serve it, it's inevitable that I will not be able to keep myself away from it. I want it for breakfast heated and drizzled with heavy cream, or I want it for dessert heated again, but this time with a scoop of rich homemade vanilla bean ice cream. The seasonal fruits in this easy show-stopper are a triple juicy threat.* SERVES 6

FILLING

4 black plums, slightly underripe, halved and cut into ½-inch slices

4 slightly underripe peaches, halved and cut into ½-inch slices

2 cups fresh blackberries

3 tablespoons granulated sugar

2 tablespoons unbleached all-purpose flour

1 tablespoon finely grated orange zest

1 teaspoon vanilla extract

1. Preheat the oven to 400°F.

2. To make the filling, lightly butter an 8-inch square baking dish. In a large bowl, combine the plums, peaches, blackberries, sugar, flour, orange zest, and vanilla and toss to mix well. Scrape the filling into the prepared baking dish and spread the top smooth.

3. To make the topping, in a medium bowl, combine the flour, brown sugar, granulated sugar, nutmeg, cinnamon, and salt and stir to mix well. Set aside. In a small saucepan over medium heat, melt the ½ cup butter.

4. Pour the melted butter into the dry topping mixture and stir to moisten evenly. Spoon the topping over the filling, covering the fruit evenly and then patting the topping into an even layer with the back of the spoon or a spatula. Dot the topping with the 2 tablespoons butter.

*continued >*

TOPPING

1¼ cups unbleached all-purpose flour

¼ cup firmly packed dark brown sugar

¼ cup granulated sugar

½ teaspoon freshly grated nutmeg

½ teaspoon ground cinnamon

¼ teaspoon salt

½ cup (1 stick) unsalted butter, plus 2 tablespoons

Vanilla Ice Cream with a Dash of Cinnamon for serving (recipe follows)

5. Bake until the topping begins to brown and the juices bubble up and become syrupy, about 40 minutes. Let cool for about 20 minutes before serving with ice cream.

# VANILLA ICE CREAM WITH A DASH OF CINNAMON

*This is my all-time tried-and-true favorite ice cream for any dessert. It's the perfect balance of simple and rich, with super-fresh vanilla flavor.* SERVES 6

1 cup whole milk

¾ cup sugar

2 cups heavy (whipping) cream

Pinch of salt

1 vanilla bean, split in half lengthwise

6 large egg yolks

1 teaspoon vanilla extract

½ teaspoon ground cinnamon

1. In a medium saucepan over low heat warm the milk, sugar, 1 cup of the cream, and the salt. Using a small knife, scrape the vanilla seeds from the bean into the milk, then add the bean pod. Remove from the heat and cover. Let the flavors meld at room temperature for 40 minutes. Remove the bean pod.

2. Pour the remaining 1 cup cream into a large bowl. In a medium bowl, whisk the egg yolks. Slowly pour the milk mixture into the egg yolks, constantly whisking until smooth. Return the egg yolk mixture to the saucepan.

3. Stir the mixture constantly over medium heat with a wooden spoon until the mixture thickens enough to coat the back of the spoon. Pour the custard through a fine-mesh sieve into a bowl, then stir in the cream. Add the vanilla extract and cinnamon, then stir. Let cool, cover, and refrigerate for 4 to 8 hours.

4. Freeze the custard mixture in an ice cream maker according to the manufacturer's directions.

# FALL

# FALL DINNER FOR 2

PEAR AND GORGONZOLA WITH FRUIT-STUDDED CRACKERS

CRISPY PORK CHOPS WITH APPLE-FIG COMPOTE

BALSAMIC BRUSSELS SPROUTS WITH TOASTED WALNUTS

BUTTERSCOTCH PUDDING

# MENU MANAGER

THE MORNING OF DINNER:

1. *Make the Butterscotch Pudding and refrigerate.*

ABOUT 3 HOURS BEFORE DINNER:

1. *Season the pork chops and refrigerate, turning occasionally.*
2. *Bring the Gorgonzola to room temperature.*

ABOUT 2 HOURS BEFORE DINNER:

1. *Make the Apple-Fig Compote and cover.*
3. *Make the Brussels sprouts and set aside at room temperature.*

JUST BEFORE YOUR GUESTS ARRIVE:

1. *Assemble the pear and cheese plate.*
2. *Set up the ingredients for the fried pork chop batter.*
3. *Remove the pork chops from the refrigerator to take the chill off.*

JUST BEFORE SERVING:

1. *Batter and fry the Crispy Pork Chops.*
2. *Gently rewarm the Brussels sprouts.*
3. *Gently rewarm the Apple-Fig Compote.*

# PEAR AND GORGONZOLA
## WITH FRUIT-STUDDED CRACKERS

*This nosh is delicious with a glass of peppery red wine before you indulge in your pork dinner. I like to use Trader Joe's Raisin Rosemary Crisps for an ideal complement. I put a large handful on the side of a decorative platter, then slice a ripe pear and place the cheese. A pretty cheese knife and, voilà, a perfect pre-dinner treat.* SERVES 2

1 large perfectly ripe Comice pear, cored and thinly sliced

4 ounces sweet Gorgonzola cheese, at room temperature (it should be ripe and nice and runny)

20 fruit-studded crackers or your favorite seedy or herb-flavored crackers

1. Choose a beautiful cheese plate or dinner plate. Arrange the ingredients attractively on the plate, also making them easy for diners to reach. Fan the pear around half the plate, heap the crackers on one side, and place the cheese in the middle, for example. Add a pretty cheese knife for spreading to add elegance to the presentation.

# CRISPY PORK CHOPS
## WITH APPLE-FIG COMPOTE

*My friend Joseph is a terrific cook who feels no meal is dinner without meat. One of his favorite dishes, and one of my favorite ways of preparing pork, is his crispy pork chops. I added a big handful of figs to his traditional apple compote to give it a little more depth and flavor and to make it a truly seasonal dish. You'll have much more of the compote than you need for serving two, but the rest will keep beautifully covered in the fridge for up to 1 week. The spice blend called quatre épices is a mix of pepper, nutmeg, cloves, and ginger; you can find it online or in gourmet and well-stocked markets.* SERVES 2

3 bone-in pork chops, each about 6 ounces and 1 inch thick, with a good layer of surrounding fat

Sea salt and freshly ground pepper

2 tablespoons fresh thyme leaves

APPLE-FIG COMPOTE

2 tablespoons unsalted butter

2 unpeeled tart apples such as Granny Smith, cored and thinly sliced

2 unpeeled sweet apples such as Gala or Honey Crisp, cored and thinly sliced

1. Rub the pork chops on both sides with salt and pepper to taste and the thyme. Refrigerate, uncovered, for 1 to 2 hours to dry, turning occasionally.

2. While the chops are drying, make the compote: In a large sauté pan or skillet, melt the butter over medium heat. Add the apples and sauté until slightly browned, 8 to 10 minutes. Add the figs and water, raise the heat to medium-high, and bring to a boil. Stir in the quatre épices, then reduce the heat to medium-low and simmer until the figs are soft, about 6 to 8 minutes. Stir in the balsamic vinegar and salt and pepper to taste. Remove from the heat and cover to keep warm.

3. About 30 minutes before frying the pork chops, remove them from the refrigerator to take the chill off. Heat the oil in a large saucepan or deep sauté pan or skillet wide enough to accommodate the chops with room to spare. (If you don't have a large enough pan, cook 1 pork chop at a time.)

8 ripe Mission (black) figs, stemmed and quartered

1½ cups water

½ teaspoon quatre épices (see recipe introduction)

3 tablespoons balsamic vinegar

Salt and freshly ground black pepper

1 cup canola or peanut oil

½ cup all-purpose flour

2 large eggs, beaten

¾ cup dried bread crumbs

4. Put the flour, the eggs, and the bread crumbs in 3 separate shallow bowls. Dredge the chops in the flour and shake off the excess. Dip into the beaten eggs, then coat with the bread crumbs.

5. When the oil is hot but not smoking, add the chops and cook on the first side until nicely browned, about 5 minutes. Flip and brown on the other side, about 5 minutes more. Transfer to paper towels to drain. Let rest for about 3 minutes.

6. Cut each chop into ¾-inch-thick slices and serve immediately with the compote.

# BALSAMIC BRUSSELS SPROUTS
## WITH TOASTED WALNUTS

*A splash of balsamic vinegar lightly caramelizes these classic roasted Brussels sprouts, bringing extra sweetness to their earthy flavor. The addition of the walnuts and fresh thyme delivers a nice crunch and an herbal finish. These tiny members of the cabbage family, roasted until tender with crisp, golden edges, are perfect with the Crispy Pork Chops (page 82), but are great as a side dish with just about anything.* SERVES 2

1 pound Brussels sprouts, trimmed and halved

1½ tablespoons olive oil, plus 2 teaspoons

1 teaspoon balsamic vinegar

1 teaspoon fresh thyme leaves

¾ teaspoon salt

½ cup walnuts

Freshly ground black pepper

1. Preheat the oven to 375°F.

2. In a medium bowl, toss together the Brussels sprouts, the 1½ tablespoons olive oil, the vinegar, thyme, and salt. Spread in a single layer on a baking sheet and set aside.

3. In a small sauté pan or skillet, warm the 2 teaspoons olive oil over medium-low heat. When the oil is hot, add the walnuts and toast, stirring often, until they become a shade darker and fragrant, about 5 minutes. Using a slotted spoon, transfer immediately to a paper towel to drain. Let cool. When cool, pour the walnuts into a large serving bowl.

4. Put the Brussels sprouts in the oven and bake for 25 minutes, or until lightly browned and tender. Move them around with a spatula about every 10 minutes, turning any that are browning quickly.

5. Add the roasted Brussels sprouts to the bowl with the walnuts, season with lots of pepper, and toss to mix. Taste for salt. Cover and set aside.

# BUTTERSCOTCH PUDDING

*This pudding is my son's favorite. He makes it a least once a month. It's ridiculously easy to create and divine every time. It's perfectly smooth in texture and pure buttery butterscotch in taste. Just remember that it needs a couple of hours to chill.* SERVES 2

¼ cup firmly packed dark brown sugar

1½ tablespoons cornstarch or arrowroot flour

¼ teaspoon salt

¾ cup whole milk

¼ cup heavy (whipping) cream

1 tablespoon unsalted butter, cut into small cubes

1 teaspoon vanilla extract

1. In a medium nonaluminum saucepan, whisk together the brown sugar, cornstarch, and salt, then whisk in the milk and cream. Bring to a boil over medium heat, whisking often. When the custard reaches a boil, whisk until smooth, about 1 minute longer. Remove from the heat and whisk in the butter and vanilla.

2. Pour the custard into 2 ramekins, dividing it evenly. Cover with plastic wrap, pressing the plastic directly onto the surface of the puddings to prevent a skin from forming. Refrigerate until set and well chilled, at least 2 hours. Serve cold.

# FALL DINNER FOR 4

SMOKED SALMON WITH PAPER-THIN FENNEL

WILD MUSHROOM RISOTTO

TREVISO SALAD WITH TOASTED ALMONDS AND GRAPEFRUIT VINAIGRETTE

FRESH FIGS WITH RICOTTA AND LAVENDER HONEY

# MENU MANAGER

THE DAY BEFORE DINNER:

1. *Make the vinaigrette and refrigerate.*
2. *Toast the almonds for the salad and store in an airtight container at room temperature.*

ABOUT 2 HOURS BEFORE DINNER:

1. *Prepare the ingredients for the salmon plate and refrigerate.*

ABOUT 1 HOUR BEFORE DINNER:

1. *Make the risotto.*

ABOUT 30 MINUTES BEFORE SERVING:

1. *Remove the vinaigrette from the fridge to bring it to room temperature.*

JUST BEFORE SERVING:

1. *Assemble and dress the Treviso salad.*

# SMOKED SALMON
## WITH PAPER-THIN FENNEL

*I like to serve this beautiful fish as a first course because it's simple and elegant. The only thing you need to be sure of is the quality of the smoked salmon. If you get terrific salmon, this is a winner. Fresh fennel is a perfect match, and slicing it paper-thin releases the delicate anise flavor as well as adding an artfulness to the presentation.* SERVES 4

1 large fennel bulb

1 pound smoked salmon, thinly sliced

2 tablespoons tiny capers, drained

1 lemon, halved lengthwise and thinly sliced crosswise

½ cup crème fraîche

2 tablespoons snipped fresh chives

Olive oil for drizzling

1. Pull the outer leaves off the fennel bulb. Wash the bulb and trim the root end. Cut off the tops, reserving 4 nice small fronds for garnish. Cut the bulb in half and cut out the tough core. Cut the fennel into very thin slices, as close to paper-thin slices as possible. If you have a mandoline, use it. Cut the slices in half to create paper-thin half-moons.

2. Arrange one-fourth of the fennel like a large fan around the edge of each of 4 small serving plates. Place several slices of the smoked salmon in the center of each plate and sprinkle with the capers. Arrange a few slices of lemon alongside the salmon and place a dollop of crème fraîche on top. Sprinkle the chives all over the plates and drizzle with the olive oil. Garnish with the reserved fennel fronds and serve immediately.

# WILD MUSHROOM RISOTTO

*This is a great vegetarian entrée if you make it with vegetable or mushroom stock. (Non-veggies can flavor it with chicken broth.) You can also serve this rich, starchy dish as a side dish for a heartier meal. Take advantage of whatever interesting mushrooms are at the market, but make sure that you mix subtle flavors with strong ones; balance is important here. For example, mix cremini with chanterelles or shiitakes, but don't mix shiitakes with chanterelles. Ask the purveyor if you're not knowledgeable about the flavors.* SERVES 4

11 cups (84 ounces) low-sodium vegetable broth or chicken broth

½ cup (1 stick) unsalted butter

¼ cup olive oil

6 large shallots, coarsely chopped

3 pounds assorted wild mushrooms such as oyster, shiitake, chanterelle, hen of the woods, and/or porcini, brushed clean and sliced

2 garlic cloves, minced

Pinch of salt

2 cups Arborio or Carnaroli rice

1. In a medium saucepan, bring the vegetable broth to a simmer over medium-high heat. Reduce the heat to very low and keep the broth warm.

2. In a large saucepan, melt the butter in the olive oil over medium-low heat. Add the shallots and sauté for 2 minutes, or until translucent. Add the mushrooms, garlic, and salt and sauté until the mushrooms are tender, they release their juices, and the liquid has reduced, about 10 minutes. Add the rice and stir to mix well and coat the grains fully with the pan juices.

3. Add the sherry and stir until the rice has fully absorbed the liquid, 5 to 8 minutes. Raise the heat to medium-high, add ½ cup of the vegetable broth, and cook, stirring often, until the liquid has been absorbed. Keep adding broth ½ cup at a time in the same manner, continuing to stir often, until the rice is tender and the mixture is creamy, 20 to 25 minutes. When you have about 1 cup of broth left,

*continued >*

1 cup dry sherry

½ cup freshly grated Parmesan cheese, plus more for garnish

½ cup freshly grated pecorino cheese, plus more for garnish

4 teaspoons minced fresh marjoram or oregano

taste the rice. If it sticks to your teeth, keep adding broth until the rice is pleasantly tender but still al dente (a little bite at the core).

4. Add the ½ cup Parmesan, the ½ cup pecorino, and the marjoram and stir for 1 minute. Divide the risotto among 4 dinner plates, garnish with more cheese, and serve immediately.

# TREVISO SALAD
## WITH TOASTED ALMONDS AND GRAPEFRUIT VINAIGRETTE

*This bitter, crunchy salad with its tart vinaigrette goes very well with the creamy texture and earthy flavor of the risotto (on page 91). Feel free to substitute walnuts or pistachios for the almonds, if you prefer. There is an abundance of vinaigrette here, to put the zest and juice of a whole grapefruit to delicious use. Store the extra dressing tightly covered in the refrigerator for up to 2 weeks.* SERVES 4

GRAPEFRUIT VINAIGRETTE

1 shallot, minced

Finely grated zest of 1 lime

Finely grated zest of 1 grapefruit

¼ cup fresh grapefruit juice

¼ cup Champagne vinegar

1 teaspoon honey

¾ cup extra-virgin olive oil

Salt and freshly ground black pepper

½ cup blanched almonds

2 large heads Treviso radicchio (about 1 pound total), halved, cored, and thinly sliced crosswise

1. To make the vinaigrette, in a medium bowl, whisk together the shallot, lime and grapefruit zests, grapefruit juice, vinegar, and honey. Slowly pour in the olive oil, whisking constantly until the dressing is well blended and creamy. Season with salt and pepper. Set aside.

2. Preheat the oven to 400°F. Spread the almonds in a pie pan and toast in the oven for 7 to 9 minutes, or until golden brown, stirring once or twice. Pour immediately onto a plate to cool. Chop coarsely and set aside.

3. In a medium bowl, toss the Treviso with about 3 tablespoons of the vinaigrette; you want the salad to be nicely coated but not overly saturated. Sprinkle with the toasted almonds and serve immediately.

# FRESH FIGS
## WITH RICOTTA AND LAVENDER HONEY

*Fall brings the arrival of big, juicy, sweet figs, and I think there is no better way to enjoy them than in simple presentations like this one featuring a crown of rich fresh ricotta cheese and a drizzle of floral honey. This dessert has both sweet and slightly salty flavors going for it, and can be assembled in minutes. As my son Lucian said while I was writing this, "Let the ingredients speak for themselves."* SERVES 4

2 cups ripe, plump fresh figs, stemmed and quartered

1 cup fresh ricotta cheese

2 tablespoons lavender honey

1. Divide the figs among 4 small dessert bowls. Scoop ¼ cup of the ricotta attractively on top of each bowl of figs. Drizzle each portion generously with honey and serve immediately.

# FALL DINNER FOR 6

CROSTINI WITH GOAT CHEESE, GARLIC, AND GRAPES

CARROT SOUP

ROASTED SPARERIBS WITH HOMEMADE BARBECUE SAUCE

SAUTÉED SPINACH WITH GARLIC AND LEMON

RUSTIC PEAR TART

# MENU MANAGER

THE DAY BEFORE DINNER:

1. *Set up the spareribs in the marinade and refrigerate, turning occasionally.*
2. *Make the dough for the pear tart and refrigerate.*
3. *Make the Carrot Soup and refrigerate.*

AT LEAST 3 HOURS OR UP TO 5 DAYS BEFORE DINNER:

1. *Make the barbecue sauce.*

ABOUT 2 HOURS BEFORE SERVING:

1. *Roast the spareribs up the point of browning under the broiler; cover tightly with foil and set aside at room temperature.*
2. *While the ribs are roasting, assemble the pear tart. When the ribs are done, reduce the oven temperature to 375°F and bake the tart.*
3. *Make the fresh mustard for the ribs.*

ABOUT 1 HOUR BEFORE YOUR GUESTS ARRIVE:

1. *When the tart is done and the oven is free again, raise the temperature to 400°F. Toast the crostini, then roast the garlic and the grape topping for the crostini together.*

JUST BEFORE YOUR GUESTS ARRIVE:

1. *Make the Sautéed Spinach and cover to keep warm.*
2. *Assemble the crostini.*
3. *Gently warm the Carrot Soup.*

JUST BEFORE SERVING:

1. *Broil the ribs for nice crispy edges.*

# CROSTINI
## WITH GOAT CHEESE, GARLIC, AND GRAPES

*These pretty bites unite three flavors that sing together. Consider making more of the roasted garlic and the grape mixture to use in divine sandwiches; they will keep, covered in the fridge, for up to 2 weeks. The grape mixture is also a terrific condiment with pork or poultry. Feel free to switch out the goat cheese with any type you like; I love this fruit-and-nut combination with ricotta. It's a bit more subtle, but also delicious.* SERVES 6

1 baguette, cut into ½-inch slices

Olive oil for brushing

2 garlic bulbs

4 cups mixed small red and green grapes

¼ cup walnuts, coarsely chopped

1½ tablespoons balsamic vinegar

About 6 ounces French goat cheese

Sea salt

1. Preheat the oven to 400°F. Arrange the baguette slices in a single layer on a baking sheet. Brush very lightly with olive oil. Toast in the oven for 5 to 7 minutes, or until golden brown. Set aside. Leave the oven on.

2. Using a serrated knife, cut off the tops of the garlic bulbs to expose the cloves. Place in a pie tin, cut side up. Set aside.

3. In a medium bowl, combine the grapes, walnuts, and vinegar and toss to mix well and coat the grapes fully with the vinegar. Transfer the mixture to a small baking dish.

4. Put the garlic and the grape mixture in the oven side by side. Bake the garlic until it is very, very soft. Bake the grape mixture until the grapes have collapsed and the juices are thick and bubbling. Both the garlic and the grapes should take 35 to 40 minutes.

5. To assemble the crostini, squeeze a roasted garlic clove from its skin onto each baguette toast. Using a small knife, spread the garlic in a smooth layer, then spread a generous teaspoon or two of the cheese on top of each. Place a spoonful of the grape mixture on top of the cheese. Arrange the crostini on a decorative platter, sprinkle with salt, and serve. If you prefer, the grape mixture is also delicious raw.

# CARROT SOUP

*This spicy, colorful carrot soup is a hit year-round, but I especially like to make it in fall to ward off the season's first chill. Rich in flavor, and inexpensive and simple to cook, it makes a lovely first course for a small crowd of six. Feel free to add more ginger if you like a hotter spicy finish.* SERVES 6

2 tablespoons unsalted butter

1 large yellow onion, chopped (about 1½ cups)

1 pound fresh, tender young carrots, peeled and sliced

2 teaspoons peeled and finely grated fresh ginger

2½ cups chicken broth

1½ teaspoons cumin seeds

1 tablespoon honey

1½ teaspoons fresh lemon juice

⅛ teaspoon ground allspice

Salt and freshly ground black pepper

½ cup whole plain yogurt

1 tablespoon minced fresh dill

1.In a saucepan, melt the butter over medium-low heat .Add the onion and sauté until soft, about 3 minutes.

2. Add the carrots and ginger and stir to release the fragrance, then pour in the chicken broth. Raise the heat to medium-high and bring to a boil, then reduce the heat to low and simmer until the vegetables are very tender, 20 to 25 minutes.

3. Meanwhile, in a small, dry skillet, toast the cumin seeds, stirring constantly, until golden, 4 to 5 minutes. Transfer to a spice grinder and process until finely ground, or grind in a mortar using a pestle.

4. Remove the soup from the heat and whisk in the honey, lemon juice, and allspice. Using a hand-held blender, process the soup in the pan to a smooth purée. (Alternatively, purée in batches in a countertop blender, transferring each batch as it is finished to a bowl. Wipe the saucepan clean and return all of the puréed soup to the pan.) Season to taste with salt and pepper.

5. Just before serving, reheat the soup gently over low heat, if necessary. Ladle the soup into warmed bowls. Dollop each serving with a heaping tablespoon of the yogurt. Sprinkle each bowl with the cumin and dill. Serve immediately.

# ROASTED SPARERIBS
## WITH HOMEMADE BARBECUE SAUCE

*Buy ribs as meaty as you can find, with a generous layer of fat, for this easy roasting technique. Ask the butcher to remove the silver skin, which is the membrane on the underside of the rack; it's tasteless and chewy in texture, and doesn't add to the flavor of the meat. Score between the ribs, so they'll be easy to carve and serve. Note that the long-simmered sauce can be made several days ahead and the ribs profit from an overnight marinating time, allowing you to keep preparation to a minimum on the day of the dinner.* SERVES 4

BARBECUE SAUCE

3 tablespoons unsalted butter

2 tablespoons olive oil

1 large sweet onion such as Vidalia, chopped

5 cups (40 ounces) ketchup

1½ cups chicken broth

3 cups water

One 28-ounce can peeled whole tomatoes, with juice

1 cup fresh orange juice with pulp

3 tablespoons ground cumin

1 to 2 tablespoons ancho chile powder (optional)

1. To make the sauce: In a large, heavy saucepan over medium heat, melt the butter in the olive oil. Add the onion and cook, stirring often, until soft, about 8 minutes. One at a time, stir in the ketchup, chicken broth, and water. Add the tomatoes with their juice, breaking up each tomato with your hands as you add them, so that they will melt gradually and lend texture to the finished sauce. Stir in the orange juice and cumin. Add the chile powder to taste if you prefer a spicier, smokier sauce. Raise the heat to medium-high and bring to a boil, then reduce the heat to low and simmer very gently until the sauce is the consistency of a thick soup, about 3 hours. (Use right away, or let cool completely and refrigerate, tightly covered, for up to 5 days, or freeze for up to 3 months.)

2. For the spareribs: Line 2 rimmed baking sheets (jelly-roll pans) with double layers of aluminum foil.

*continued* >

SPARERIBS

Leaves from 1 bunch fresh oregano

¼ cup olive oil, plus more for basting

Coarse sea salt and freshly ground black pepper

2 full racks of pork spareribs (about 4½ pounds total)

FRESH MUSTARD

3 tablespoons dry mustard

Pinch of salt

3 teaspoons apple cider vinegar, or as needed

3. In a small bowl, stir together the oregano, the ¼ cup olive oil, and salt and pepper to taste. Rub the mixture all over the ribs. Place one rack of ribs on each prepared baking sheet and cover tightly with another large piece of foil. Let marinate at cool room temperature for at least 1 hour or, preferably, refrigerate for up to 24 hours, turning the ribs occasionally.

4. Position one rack on the top rung of the oven and a second rack underneath it as high as possible allowing room for a pan of ribs, and preheat to 500°F. Remove the foil from the ribs and turn bone side up. Place one pan of ribs on each of the upper oven racks and roast for 15 minutes. Remove from the oven and baste with olive oil; be careful, as the pan will be very hot! Return to the oven for another 15 minutes, then remove again, flip the ribs meaty side up, and baste with the pan drippings. Return to the oven again and roast until the meat is tender and soft, about 30 minutes longer. Remove from the oven and set aside.

5. To make the fresh mustard, in a small bowl, stir together the mustard powder, salt, and vinegar as needed to make a smooth, liquid paste. Set aside.

6. To serve the ribs, preheat the broiler and gently rewarm the barbecue sauce, if necessary. Turn the ribs bone side up. One at a time, slip a pan of ribs under the hot broiler and broil until just starting to brown, 2 to 3 minutes. Remove from the broiler and flip meaty side up. Broil until the second side starts to brown, 2 to 3 minutes longer. Remove from the broiler again, brush with the barbecue sauce, and return to the broiler. Keep close watch and remove just as the ribs are starting to char and get crispy at the edges. Set aside and cover with foil to keep warm. Repeat with the second pan of ribs. Carve the meat off the ribs and serve immediately, with piping hot barbecue sauce and fresh mustard on the side.

# SAUTÉED SPINACH
## WITH GARLIC AND LEMON

*My feeling is, if a leafy side dish is wilted, green, and garlicky, it's the perfect addition to any meal. I enjoy this rendition as an accompaniment to ribs, because the fresh and clean flavors help to balance out the rich meat and tangy, heavily spiced sauce.* SERVES 6

3 tablespoons olive oil

6 garlic cloves, chopped (about 2 tablespoons)

1½ pounds spinach, tough stems removed

2 teaspoons kosher salt

¾ teaspoon freshly ground black pepper

½ lemon

1. In a large sauté pan or skillet, heat the olive oil over medium heat. When the oil is hot, add the garlic and sauté until fragrant, about 1 minute. Add the spinach, salt, and pepper and stir to mix well. Cover and cook for 3 minutes.

2. Uncover the pan, raise the heat to high, and cook, stirring and tossing as needed, until all of the spinach is wilted, about 1 minute longer. Transfer to a serving bowl, squeeze the lemon half on top, and serve immediately.

# RUSTIC PEAR TART

*The great thing about rustic tarts is that they're meant to be homemade and imperfect, so there's no need to worry if one looks technically unlovely—it will still be gorgeous! This tart is delicious topped with crème fraîche, fresh whipped cream, or vanilla ice cream.* SERVES 6

CRUST

1⅓ cups unbleached all-purpose flour, plus more for dusting

3 tablespoons sugar

¼ teaspoon salt

7 tablespoons cold butter, cut into small cubes

2 to 3 tablespoons ice water

1. To make the crust, in a medium bowl, whisk together the flour, sugar, and salt. Add the butter pieces and toss to coat and distribute. Using a pastry blender or 2 knives, cut in the butter until the mixture is uniformly crumbly, with no pieces bigger than a pea. Add the ice water slowly while tossing gently with a fork; add only enough of the water to moisten the mixture fully. Then, using your fingers, press the dough into a disk about 4 inches in diameter. Wrap tightly in plastic wrap and refrigerate until well chilled, at least 2 hours or up to overnight.

2. At least 2 hours before you want to serve your tart, preheat the oven to 375°F.

3. Remove the dough from the refrigerator, unwrap, and let soften for about 15 minutes. Place on a lightly floured work surface and roll out into a round about 14 inches in diameter, dusting the dough, the rolling pin, or the work surface with more flour as needed to prevent sticking. Transfer the dough round to a baking sheet.

*continued >*

FILLING

¾ cup sugar

¼ cup unbleached all-purpose flour

2 teaspoons finely grated orange zest

1 to 2 teaspoons fresh lemon juice

½ teaspoon ground cinnamon

¼ teaspoon ground nutmeg

Pinch of salt

4 medium ripe pears, peeled, cored, cut into¼-inch slices

1 tablespoon unsalted butter

1 large egg

1 teaspoon water

1 tablespoon coarse sugar

4. To make the filling, in a large bowl, whisk together the sugar, flour, orange zest, lemon juice, cinnamon, nutmeg, and salt. Add the pears and toss until coated. Spread the filling on the pastry round, leaving a 3-inch border uncovered. Fold the edges of the pastry up over the filling, creating pleats to take up the extra dough; the filling will not be completely covered. Dot the crust with the butter for an extra golden touch.

5. In a small bowl, beat together the egg and water. Brush the pastry with the egg wash and sprinkle with the coarse sugar. Bake for 50 to 60 minutes, or until the crust is golden brown and the juices are bubbling. Let cool on the pan for about 15 minutes. Using a wide spatula, slide the tart onto a serving dish. Cut into wedges and serve warm.

WINTER

# WINTER DINNER FOR 2

CLASSIC OLD FASHIONED COCKTAILS

RIB-EYE STEAK ON GARLICKY WINTER GREENS

ROASTED NEW POTATOES WITH ROSEMARY

SUNDAES WITH CHOCOLATE SAUCE AND SALTED WALNUTS

# MENU MANAGER

THE DAY BEFORE DINNER:

1. *Make the ice cream.*
2. *Make the chocolate sauce and toasted walnuts for the sundaes.*

ABOUT 1 HOUR BEFORE YOUR GUESTS ARRIVE:

1. *Remove the steak from the refrigerator; season and let come to room temperature.*
2. *Prepare the garlic and greens for the Garlicky Winter Greens.*

JUST BEFORE SERVING:

1. *Cook and assemble the steaks and greens.*
2. *Roast the potatoes.*

JUST BEFORE SERVING DESSERT:

1. *Gently reheat the chocolate sauce.*

# CLASSIC OLD FASHIONED COCKTAILS

*I really like the no-nonsense taste of this boozy cocktail. There are several stories about the origins of the Old Fashioned, but the one that seems most plausible to me is that "Old Fashioned" was the name of a bourbon that was popular at the Pendennis Club in Louisville, Kentucky. The cocktail was created by a bartender at the club, and a club member and bourbon distiller brought the recipe to the Waldorf-Astoria Hotel in New York, where the drink became a classic overnight.* SERVES 2

2 sugar cubes

2 dashes bitters

2 teaspoons water

4 fresh cherries

4 slices lemon

4 slices orange

4 ounces bourbon

Ice cubes

1. In each of 2 Old Fashioned glasses, put 1 sugar cube, 1 dash of bitters, 1 teaspoon water, 2 fresh cherries, 2 thin lemon slices, and 2 thin orange slices. Muddle all of the ingredients together until roughly broken up and fragrant. Add the whiskey and stir. Add a few ice cubes to each and stir again.

2. Garnish each glass with 2 lemon slices and 2 orange slices, top with a cherry, and serve.

# RIB-EYE STEAK
## ON GARLICKY WINTER GREENS

*To me, there's no better cut of beef than a bone-in rib-eye—I'm a woman who likes meat that's juicy but with a little bit of chew. Bone-in rib-eye has the marbled fat that makes meat juicy and flavorful and also gives it texture. This is a perfect steak for sharing, and if you love the bone, as I do, share that, too!* SERVES 2

1 bone-in rib-eye steak, about 1½ pounds and 1½ inches thick

3¼ teaspoons sea salt

Freshly ground black pepper

3½ tablespoons olive oil

3 large garlic cloves, thinly sliced

1 head radicchio, halved, cored, and thinly sliced

2 bunches watercress, stemmed

2 bunches fresh spinach, stemmed, leaves cut in half crosswise

½ lemon

1. Season the meat on both sides with 3 teaspoons of the salt and generous amounts of pepper. Place a large cast-iron skillet over high heat, add 1½ tablespoons of the oil, and heat until the oil begins to smoke. Add the steak and press with a spatula so that the meat makes contact with the pan evenly. Cook, turning once, for 6 minutes per side for medium-rare or 8 minutes per side for medium. Transfer to a cutting board and let rest for 5 minutes.

2. While the meat is cooking, in a large sauté pan or skillet, and heat the remaining 2 tablespoons olive oil over medium-high heat for 2 minutes. Add the garlic and sauté until lightly golden. Add the radicchio, watercress, spinach, and remaining ¼ teaspoon salt and stir for 2 to 3 minutes, then cover and steam for 5 minutes, or until all the greens are fully wilted. Just before serving, squeeze the lemon over the greens and taste for salt and pepper.

3. To serve, carve the steak across the grain on the diagonal into thin slices. Make a bed of the garlic greens on each plate and divide the steak between them, arranging the slices on top of the greens.

# ROASTED NEW POTATOES
## WITH ROSEMARY

*These potatoes are crispy on the outside and soft and tender inside. I can have them for dinner with a side of spinach and be completely satisfied, but they also go really well with any kind of beef, poultry, or fish. I add rosemary in this recipe, but they're also wonderful with fresh thyme.* SERVES 2

1½ pounds baby new potatoes, scrubbed but not peeled, quartered

2 tablespoons olive oil

½ teaspoon sea salt

½ teaspoon freshly ground pepper

2 teaspoons minced fresh rosemary

1. Preheat the oven to 425°F.

2. Put the potatoes in a bowl and drizzle them with the olive oil. Add the salt, pepper, and rosemary and toss to coat evenly.

3. Spread the potatoes on a rimmed baking sheet (jelly-roll pan) in a single layer, making sure that none of them are touching to ensure that the skins crisp evenly.

4. Roast for 20 minutes, or until golden brown on top. Toss them around with a metal spatula and cook until nicely browned all over and tender when pierced with a knife, about 10 minutes longer.

5. Transfer the potatoes to a shallow serving bowl and serve immediately.

# SUNDAES
## WITH CHOCOLATE SAUCE AND SALTED WALNUTS

*This may look like a massive undertaking for a dessert for two, but the recipe makes enough so that you can make several sundaes for another evening or if guests join you for dessert. While there's nothing better than homemade ice cream with homemade chocolate sauce, if you're rushed, get a good-quality vanilla ice cream and just make the sauce and the nuts. You'll still have a wonderful dessert that's a close second to one that's entirely homemade.* SERVES 2

SALTED TOASTED WALNUTS

1 cup walnut halves

2 egg whites, slightly whipped

2 teaspoons sea salt

Vanilla Ice Cream with a Dash of Cinnamon (page 75)

Bittersweet Chocolate Sauce (page 51)

1. To make the nuts, preheat the oven to 400°F and line a baking sheet with aluminum foil. In a medium bowl, toss the walnuts with the egg whites and salt until the nuts are completely coated. Spread the nuts in a single layer on the prepared pan. Toast in the oven for 10 to 12 minutes, or until golden, stirring once or twice. Let cool on the pan for 15 minutes, then transfer to a plate and set aside.

2. Gently rewarm the chocolate sauce if necessary. To assemble the sundaes, place 2 scoops of ice cream in each bowl. Spoon the chocolate sauce generously over the ice cream, sprinkle the salted walnuts over the top, and serve.

# WINTER DINNER FOR 4

FRESH OYSTERS WITH MIGNONETTE SAUCE

BRANZINO STUFFED WITH LEEKS, PARSLEY, AND LEMON

CAULIFLOWER GRATIN

HAZELNUT SHORTBREAD

# MENU MANAGER

THE DAY BEFORE DINNER:

1. *Make the shortbread dough and refrigerate.*

THE MORNING OF DINNER:

1. *Bake the shortbread.*
2. *Make the Cauliflower Gratin up to the final browning step. Cover and refrigerate.*

ABOUT 2 HOURS BEFORE SERVING:

1. *Make the Mignonette Sauce and refrigerate.*
2. *Season and stuff the branzini and set them up in the roasting pan; refrigerate.*

JUST BEFORE YOUR GUESTS ARRIVE:

1. *Shuck the oysters, if necessary, and refrigerate on a platter on the half-shell.*

ABOUT 30 MINUTES BEFORE SERVING:

1. *Remove the gratin from the fridge to take the chill off; uncover.*
2. *While the fish is resting, add the cheese and bread crumbs to the gratin and finish baking.*

JUST BEFORE SERVING:

1. *Bake the fish.*

# FRESH OYSTERS
## WITH MIGNONETTE SAUCE

*Light, full of transporting mineral flavors, and scrumptious, oysters make any meal special. There are so many wonderful and wonderfully different varieties, depending on where you live (of course, West Coast oysters are available for purchase on the East Coast and vice versa). Everyone has their favorites. I prefer the milky, plump ones to the briny ones, but I know plenty of people who like the briny, thinner ones. Choose the ones you like best and pair them with this tangy mignonette. Have your fishmonger shuck the oysters for you, if you prefer not to wrestle with an oyster knife.* SERVES 4

MIGNONETTE SAUCE

1 tablespoon coarsely ground white pepper

½ cup Champagne vinegar

2 large shallots, minced

1 teaspoon minced fresh flat-leaf (Italian) parsley

Large pinch of sea salt

24 fresh oysters or fresh cherrystone clams, on the half-shell

1. To make the mignonette, in a small bowl, whisk together all the ingredients. Cover the sauce and refrigerate until well chilled, at least 1 hour or up to 2 hours.

2. To serve, pour the mignonette into 4 tiny bowls and place one at each diner's place. Arrange the oysters on a chilled platter or a bed of ice and serve immediately, placing them in the center of the table.

# BRANZINO
## STUFFED WITH LEEKS, PARSLEY, AND LEMON

*The first time I had branzino was at a restaurant in New York City called Market Table. They served a whole branzino per person, stuffed with fennel, parsley, and lemon. The dish was light even though it was filling, and the flesh of the fish was succulent and sweet. I loved everything about that delicious recipe. Here's my version.* SERVES 4

Four 1-pound whole branzini, scaled and gutted by the fishmonger

Salt and freshly ground black pepper

3 large leeks, white parts only, thinly sliced and rinsed well

1 bunch fresh flat-leaf (Italian) parsley

1 lemon, thinly sliced

2 tablespoons olive oil, plus more for drizzling

1 cup dry white wine

1. Preheat the oven to 475°F.

2. Season the fish cavities with salt and pepper. Stuff each cavity with the leeks, a small handful of parsley, and 2 slices of lemon.

3. Pour the 2 tablespoons olive oil into a large roasting pan. Place all 4 fish in the oiled pan, spacing them so they are not touching. Drizzle with more olive oil and sprinkle with salt and pepper. Pour the white wine over all.

4. Roast until the fish is cooked all the way through but is tender and flakes easily, 10 to 15 minutes. Using a fish spatula or other wide spatula, transfer to a large serving platter. Pour the pan juices over the fish, garnish with more lemon slices and fresh parsley, and serve immediately.

# CAULIFLOWER GRATIN

*If you're a fan of potato gratins, you'll love this version using winter's boon, the sturdy cauliflower. It's a delicious alternative to the classic. You don't have to add the bread crumbs, but I like to because I love any kind of crust, and the crumbs guarantee a crispy, cheesy, crunchy top.* SERVES 4

1 large head of cauliflower (about 3 pounds), cut into florets

4 tablespoons unsalted butter

3 tablespoons all-purpose flour

2 cups milk

1 teaspoon fresh marjoram leaves or 2 teaspoons chopped fresh flat-leaf (Italian) parsley

¼ teaspoon freshly grated nutmeg

1 teaspoon sea salt

Freshly ground black pepper

1 cup shredded Gruyère cheese

¼ cup grated Parmesan cheese

¼ cup dried bread crumbs

1. Preheat the oven to 475°F. Butter an 8-inch square baking dish.

2. In a steamer basket over 1 inch of boiling water, cook the cauliflower for 5 minutes, or until tender. Rinse the cauliflower under cold running water to stop the cooking, then drain thoroughly and pat dry. Set aside.

3. In a medium saucepan over medium heat, melt the butter. Whisk in the flour until a smooth paste forms. Slowly pour in the milk, whisking constantly. When the milk mixture begins to simmer, reduce the heat to medium-low and cook until the sauce is thickened and creamy, about 5 minutes. Remove from the heat and stir in the marjoram, nutmeg, salt, and pepper to taste.

4. Add the cauliflower to the sauce and stir until the florets are coated. Transfer to the prepared baking dish. Bake, uncovered, for 10 minutes. To make ahead, remove from the oven and let stand at room temperature for up to 8 hours, or let cool, cover, and refrigerate for up to 2 days (bring to room temperature before proceeding with the recipe). To serve, in a medium bowl, stir together the cheeses and bread crumbs and sprinkle over the gratin. Bake in a preheated 475°F oven until golden and bubbling, about 5 minutes. Serve hot.

# HAZELNUT SHORTBREAD

*This cookie is one that even people who are not crazy for sweets love. The buttery confection is divine dipped in hot chocolate or into a nice, stiff black espresso.* MAKES 40 COOKIES

½ cup hazelnuts

1½ cups (3 sticks) unsalted butter, at room temperature

1 cup sugar

¾ teaspoon vanilla extract or orange extract

3½ cups unbleached all-purpose flour

½ teaspoon salt

1. Preheat the oven to 400°F. Spread the hazelnuts in a pie pan and toast in the oven until golden brown, about 7 minutes. Wrap in a towel and rub to remove the skins. Chop finely and set aside.

2. In a large bowl, combine the butter and sugar. Using an electric mixer, beat on medium speed until smooth and completely blended. Beat in the vanilla. Add the flour, salt, and toasted nuts, reduce the speed to low, and beat until a rough dough forms. Turn the dough out onto a work surface and press it into a disk. Wrap tightly in plastic wrap and refrigerate for at least 30 minutes or up to overnight.

3. An hour before baking, remove the dough from the fridge. Preheat the oven to 325°F.

4. Roll the dough out on a lightly floured work surface to a thickness of about ½ inch. Cut into 2-inch triangles or finger-shaped cookies. Place on an ungreased baking sheet about 1 inch apart. Bake for 25 to 30 minutes, or until the bottoms are lightly browned. Transfer the pan to a wire rack and let cool completely. Repeat to bake the remaining cookies. Store in an airtight container, separating layers with wax paper, for up to 2 weeks.

# WINTER DINNER FOR 6

BRAISED BEEF WITH CARROTS AND ONIONS

WHIPPED PARSNIPS

CHOPPED WINTER GREENS WITH FUYU PERSIMMONS AND ORANGE VINAIGRETTE

FRESH-GINGER BUNDT CAKE WITH SWEETENED WHIPPED CREAM

HOT TODDIES

# MENU MANAGER

THE DAY BEFORE DINNER:

1. *Put the beef in the marinade and refrigerate.*

THE MORNING OF DINNER:

1. *Make the cake and set aside at room temperature.*
2. *Make the vinaigrette and refrigerate.*
3. *Prepare the ingredients for the salad and refrigerate.*

ABOUT 4 HOURS BEFORE DINNER:

1. *Brown the beef, prepare the sauce and vegetables for the pan, and put the roast in the oven.*

ABOUT 1 HOUR BEFORE YOUR GUESTS ARRIVE:

1. *Make the Whipped Parsnips and cover to keep warm.*
2. *Make the whipped cream and refrigerate.*
3. *Remove the vinaigrette from the fridge to bring it to room temperature.*

JUST BEFORE SERVING:

1. *Gently reheat the parsnips, if necessary.*
2. *Assemble and dress the salad.*

# BRAISED BEEF
## WITH CARROTS AND ONIONS

*There are so many cuts of meat that lend themselves to the kind of slow cooking in this recipe. Some people love a beef brisket or a round roast; others say go with a beef flat iron, as it never gets stringy. I've tried them all and find that a beef flat iron from the shoulder is the best of the bunch (unless you're partial to that stringy texture, to which I say, all power to you, and go ahead and use a brisket for the flat iron called for here). You'll likely need to order the flat iron shoulder roast ahead of time; ask your butcher. This stew gets better with time, so this recipe makes enough for leftovers.* SERVES 6

MARINADE

5 to 7 garlic cloves, smashed

2 fresh rosemary sprigs

¼ cup olive oil

2 teaspoons sea salt

1 bay leaf

1 dried red chile

Grated zest of ½ orange

Juice of 1 orange

1 beef flat iron roast (about 5 pounds), skin removed but with a good layer of surrounding fat

1. To make the marinade, in a large shallow dish, combine all of the ingredients. Place the meat in the mixture and flip it a couple of times to coat completely. Cover tightly with plastic wrap and place it in the refrigerator. Let marinate overnight, turning occasionally.

2. Preheat the oven to 350°F.

3. Remove the meat from the marinade and set aside. Transfer the marinade to a food processor and process to a coarse purée, or run through a food mill. Set aside.

4. Pour the ¼ cup olive oil into a large flameproof roasting pan or Dutch oven and place over medium-high heat. Add the roast and sear to brown on all sides, 8 to 10 minutes total. Transfer the beef to a plate and set aside.

5. Discard the olive oil in the pan, wipe the pan clean, and add the 2 tablespoons olive oil. Heat the oil over medium-low heat. When the oil is warm, add the onions, carrots, and garlic and sauté until the onions are translucent, 8 to 10 minutes. Add the wine and

¼ cup olive oil, plus 2 tablespoons

15 cippolini onions, peeled but left whole

8 small carrots, peeled and cut into 2-inch chunks

4 garlic cloves, quartered lengthwise

2 cups rich, dry but fruity red wine such as Syrah or Burgundy

3 cups beef broth

Sea salt and freshly ground black pepper

Wipped Parsnips (page 132) for serving

stir to scrape up any browned bits from the pan bottom. Cook until the wine is thoroughly blended with the pan juices and the flavors have married, about 10 minutes. Stir in the beef broth, bring to a simmer, and cook until the liquid is reduced by half, about 10 minutes longer. Stir in the puréed marinade and salt and pepper to taste. Nestle the roast in the sauce and cover the pan with aluminum foil or a lid. Transfer to the oven and roast until very tender, 2½ to 3 hours, turning the beef about halfway through the cooking time.

6. To serve, carve the beef across the grain on the diagonal into thin slices. Arrange the slices on each plate over a scoop of the parsnips. Spoon the pan sauce over the beef, giving each diner some of the onions and carrots, and serve immediately.

# WHIPPED PARSNIPS

*Parsnips, a sometimes overlooked sweet root vegetable, are a great substitute for mashed potatoes. They whip up smooth and creamy, and the addition of Dijon mustard gives them a nice touch of tangy bite. Add more mustard if you'd like the mash to be a bit spicier.* SERVES 6

2 pounds parsnips, peeled, halved lengthwise, and cut into 2-inch chunks

Sea salt and freshly ground black pepper

3 cups whole milk

4 tablespoons unsalted butter

1 tablespoon Dijon mustard

2 tablespoons minced fresh flat-leaf (Italian) parsley

1. In a large saucepan, combine the parsnips and a pinch of salt. Pour in the milk and bring to a boil over high heat. Reduce the heat to medium-low and simmer until the parsnips are tender when pierced with a fork, 12 to 14 minutes.

2. Using a slotted spoon, transfer the parsnip mixture to a blender or food processor and add the butter and mustard. Add about ¾ cup of the milk from the pan and process until smooth. Keep adding milk a little at a time, just as needed to give the purée a nice creamy, smooth texture, while retaining the volume and not making it too soft or liquidy. Also be careful not to overprocess, or the mash may become gluey.

3. Season with salt and pepper and transfer to plates or a serving dish. Garnish with the parsley and serve.

# CHOPPED WINTER GREENS
## WITH FUYU PERSIMMONS AND ORANGE VINAIGRETTE

*Any winter green will work well with the persimmons. The sweetness of the persimmons and the dressing is a perfect contrast to the crunchy bitterness of the greens.* SERVES 6

VINAIGRETTE

Grated zest of 1 orange

Juice of 2 oranges

2 tablespoons Champagne vinegar

1 tablespoon honey

1 teaspoon Dijon mustard

1 garlic clove, minced

¾ cup extra-virgin olive oil

Sea salt and freshly ground pepper

2 heads frisée, hearts only

2 small heads escarole, cored

2 endives, cored and quartered

3 ripe but firm Fuyu persimmons

1. To make the vinaigrette, in a small bowl, whisk together the orange zest and juice, vinegar, honey, mustard, and garlic. Slowly pour in the olive oil, whisking constantly until the dressing is well blended and creamy. Season with salt and pepper.

2. Break the frisée into pieces. Chop the escarole and cut the endives on the diagonal into thin slices. Peel, core, and thinly slice the persimmons.

3. Just before serving, combine the greens and persimmons in a large bowl and toss to mix. Add the vinaigrette to taste and toss gently to coat. Serve immediately. (Store any remaining vinaigrette tightly covered in the refrigerator for up to 1 month.)

# FRESH-GINGER BUNDT CAKE
## WITH SWEETENED WHIPPED CREAM

*If you're a ginger lover, this is your dessert! This super-moist cake is lovely for breakfast, too. Enjoy it with whipped cream, or top with a scoop of vanilla ice cream instead. Using both fresh ginger and ground ginger gives the cake a full, singing, spicy ginger flavor.* SERVES 10

2½ cups unbleached all-purpose flour

4 teaspoons baking powder

4 teaspoons ground ginger

1¼ teaspoons ground cinnamon

½ teaspoon fine sea salt

1 cup (2 sticks) unsalted butter, at room temperature

1¼ cups packed brown sugar

¼ cup peeled and grated fresh ginger

4 large eggs, at room temperature

1 teaspoon vanilla extract

1 cup milk

1. Preheat the oven to 350°F.

2. Lightly butter a 12-cup Bundt pan. Dust with flour and tap out the excess.

3. In a medium bowl, sift together the flour, baking powder, ground ginger, cinnamon, and salt. Set aside.

4. In a large bowl, using an electric mixer on medium speed, beat the butter, brown sugar, and fresh ginger until pale and fluffy. Beat in the eggs, one at a time, and then the vanilla. Add the flour mixture in 3 batches alternately with the milk in 2 batches, scraping the bottom of the bowl well after each addition. Spread the batter evenly in the prepared pan.

5. Bake for 45 minutes, or until a long toothpick inserted in the center comes out clean. Rotate the pan halfway through the baking time. Transfer to a wire rack and let cool in the pan completely.

SWEETENED WHIPPED CREAM

1 cup heavy (whipping) cream

1 teaspoon granulated sugar

½ cup candied ginger, finely chopped

6. For the whipped cream: Just before serving, using a whisk or an electric mixer, combine the cream and granulated sugar in a bowl and whisk or beat until medium-stiff peaks form.

7. To serve, invert the pan onto a serving plate and unmold the cake. Cut into wedges and serve, topped with the whipped cream and a sprinkling of the candied ginger.

# HOT TODDIES

*Serve this cozy classic drink with dessert. Its fragrance is intoxicating, and its taste is boozy, tart, and slightly sweet all at once. One sip fills your chest with warmth. The perfect end to any winter meal!* SERVES 6

6 ounces bourbon

6 tablespoons honey, preferably clover

12 teaspoons fresh lemon juice

6 cloves

6 small cinnamon sticks

7½ cups boiling water

½ lemon, thinly sliced

1. Put 1 ounce of bourbon, 1 tablespoon honey, 2 teaspoons lemon juice, 1 clove, and 1 cinnamon stick in each of 6 large mugs. Top off each with the boiling water (about 1¼ cups per mug) and stir until the honey is dissolved. Garnish each mug with a lemon slice and serve.

# INDEX

## D



## E



## F



## G

## Q



## R



## S

# TABLE OF EQUIVALENTS

The exact equivalents in the following tables have been rounded for convenience.

## LIQUID/DRY MEASUREMENTS

| U.S. | Metric |
|---|---|
| ¼ teaspoon | 1.25 milliliters |
| ½ teaspoon | 2.5 milliliters |
| 1 teaspoon | 5 milliliters |
| 1 tablespoon (3 teaspoons) | 15 milliliters |
| 1 fluid ounce (2 tablespoons) | 30 milliliters |
| ¼ cup | 60 milliliters |
| ⅓ cup | 80 milliliters |
| ½ cup | 120 milliliters |
| 1 cup | 240 milliliters |
| 1 pint (2 cups) | 480 milliliters |
| 1 quart (4 cups, 32 ounces) | 960 milliliters |
| 1 gallon (4 quarts) | 3.84 liters |
| | |
| 1 ounce (by weight) | 28 grams |
| 1 pound | 454 grams |
| 2.2 pounds | 1 kilogram |

## LENGTHS

| U.S. | Metric |
|---|---|
| ⅛ inch | 3 millimeters |
| ¼ inch | 6 millimeters |
| ½ inch | 12 millimeters |
| 1 inch | 2.5 centimeters |

## OVEN TEMPERATURE

| Fahrenheit | Celsius | Gas |
|---|---|---|
| 250 | 120 | ½ |
| 275 | 140 | 1 |
| 300 | 150 | 2 |
| 325 | 160 | 3 |
| 350 | 180 | 4 |
| 375 | 190 | 5 |
| 400 | 200 | 6 |
| 425 | 220 | 7 |
| 450 | 230 | 8 |
| 475 | 240 | 9 |
| 500 | 260 | 10 |